PowerShell Source Code: Using Get-CIMInstance

By Richard Thomas Edwards

CONTENTS

INTRODUCTION

Why another book on PowerShell?

I really put some thought into that question. For about 2 minutes and then started to write it.

Fact is, I don't need a reason for writing this book. Because it really isn't a book, it is 100 pages of source code you simply can't afford to not to use.

I'm not saying you have to buy my book, I'm saying that the reason why I am writing this book is because, like you, I was once in your shoes looking for that one perfect example no how to get through a sticky point in my coding experience that not only worked for me, it worked for my customers who were developers and being supported by Microsoft Technical Support.

Back then, that single chapter, that one little piece of information, cost me $50. Today, you're looking at being able to get the same for a measily $3.99 for the E-book and around $14.95 for the Paperback.

The problem that I have is, in order to fill 100 pages, I have to use the same routines across every other book I am writing. Otherwise, you don't get a nice size book of coding examples and I don't get paid enough money to cover my time and effort producing these books.

So, please excuse the canned content that I've added as example code using Get-WMIObject. It is needed to give you that kernel of code you will need to make the code work for you.

WHAT WMI NAMESPACES AND CLASSES ARE ON YOUR MACHINE?

Someone once said, "It is what you don't know that can kill you," Well, they might not have said it exactly that way, but you get the idea.

How can you use something that exists on your machine, but you don't know it?

Back in 2002, I created something called the WMI Explorer. Microsoft came out with their version in May of 2003. Neither one of us cared, It pretty much fell flat on its face.

The biggest difference between the two is my class groupings was based on the way the classes were presented. In-other-words, I there was no underscore, the category was the classname. If there was an underscore at the beginning of the classname, it was a superclass. It there was an underscore in the middle of the classname, the letters before the underscore became its category.

I thought it was a pretty good idea at the time.

Apparently, no one else did. Fact is, the concept was never used by anyone else and WMI Explorer that other people began to "create" used the Microsoft template and never did consider a more granular approach.

I also think the other reason why the WMI Explorer didn't become popular was because of the lack of documentation beyond the most common root: root\cimv2. And back in 2003 time, there were less than a few hundred of them.

But today is a completely different ballpark. Today there are literally hundreds of classes under root\cimv2 alone.

Would you like your own personal copy?

The following scripts that I've been using since 2002, will make that happen for you. Just create a folder on your desktop, then copy and paste the three scripts into that directory and start with namespaces.vbs and end with classes.vbs.

NAMESPACES.VBS

```
Dim fso
Dim l
Dim s


EnumNamespaces("root")

Sub EnumNamespaces(ByVal nspace)

Set ws = CreateObject("Wscript.Shell")
Set fso = CreateObject("Scripting.FilesystemObject")

If fso.folderExists(ws.currentDirectory & "\" & nspace) = false then
 fso.CreateFolder(ws.currentDirectory & "\" & nspace)
End If

On error Resume Next

Set objs = GetObject("Winmgmts:\\.\" & nspace).InstancesOf("___Namespace",
&H20000)

If err.Number <> 0 Then
 err.Clear
 Exit Sub
End If

For each obj in objs
   EnumNamespaces(nspace & "\" & obj.Name)
Next

End Sub
```

Categories.VBS

```vbs
Dim fso
Dim l
Dim s

Set ws = CreateObject("Wscript.Shell")
Set fso = CreateObject("Scripting.FilesystemObject")

EnumNamespaces("root")


Sub EnumNamespaces(ByVal nspace)

EnumCategories(nspace)

If fso.folderExists(ws.currentDirectory & "\" & nspace) = false then
  fso.CreateFolder(ws.currentDirectory & "\" & nspace)
End If

On error Resume Next

Set       objs       =       GetObject("Winmgmts:\\.\"       &
nspace).InstancesOf("___Namespace", &H20000)

If err.Number <> 0 Then
  err.Clear
  Exit Sub
End If

For each obj in objs

  EnumNamespaces(nspace & "\" & obj.Name)

Next

End Sub

Sub EnumCategories(ByVal nspace)
```

```vbs
Set ws = CreateObject("Wscript.Shell")
Set fso = CreateObject("Scripting.FilesystemObject")

Set objs = GetObject("Winmgmts:\\.\" & nspace).SubClassesOf("", &H20000)
For each obj in objs

    pos = instr(obj.Path_.class, "_")

    if pos = 0 then
        If  fso.folderExists(ws.currentDirectory  &  "\"  &  nspace  &  "\"  &
obj.Path_.Class) = false then
            fso.CreateFolder(ws.currentDirectory  &  "\"  &  nspace  &  "\"  &
obj.Path_.Class)
        End If
    else
        if pos = 1 then
            If  fso.folderExists(ws.currentDirectory  &  "\"  &  nspace  &
"\SuperClasses") = false then
                fso.CreateFolder(ws.currentDirectory  &  "\"  &  nspace  &
"\SuperClasses")
            End If
        else
            If  fso.folderExists(ws.currentDirectory  &  "\"  &  nspace  &  "\"  &
Mid(obj.Path_.Class, 1, pos-1)) = false then
                fso.CreateFolder(ws.currentDirectory  &  "\"  &  nspace  &  "\"  &
Mid(obj.Path_.Class, 1, pos-1))
            End If
        End If
    End If

Next

End Sub
```

Classes.VBS

```vbs
Dim fso
```

```
Dim l
Dim s

EnumNamespaces("root")

Sub EnumNamespaces(ByVal nspace)

EnumClasses(nspace)

Set ws = CreateObject("Wscript.Shell")
Set fso = CreateObject("Scripting.FilesystemObject")

If fso.folderExists(ws.currentDirectory & "\" & nspace) = false then
  fso.CreateFolder(ws.currentDirectory & "\" & nspace)
End If

On error Resume Next

Set       objs       =       GetObject("Winmgmts:\\.\"       &
nspace).InstancesOf("___Namespace", &H20000)

If err.Number <> 0 Then
  err.Clear
  Exit Sub
End If

For each obj in objs

    EnumNamespaces(nspace & "\" & obj.Name)

Next

End Sub

Sub EnumClasses(ByVal nspace)

Set ws = CreateObject("Wscript.Shell")
Set fso = CreateObject("Scripting.FilesystemObject")

Set objs = GetObject("Winmgmts:\\.\" & nspace).SubClassesOf("", &H20000)
```

```
For each obj in objs

    pos = instr(obj.Path_.class, "_")

    if pos = 0 then
        call  CreateXMLFile(ws.CurrentDirectory  &  "\"  &  nspace  &  "\"  &
obj.Path_.Class, nspace, obj.Path_.Class)
    else
      if pos = 1 then
        call    CreateXMlFile(ws.CurrentDirectory    &    "\"    &    nspace    &
"\Superclasses", nspace, obj.Path_.Class)
        else
          call  CreateXMLFile(ws.CurrentDirectory  &  "\"  &  nspace  &  "\"  &
Mid(obj.Path_.Class, 1, pos-1), nspace, obj.Path_.Class)
        End If
      End If

  Next

End Sub

Sub CreateXMLFile(ByVal Path, ByVal nspace, ByVal ClassName)



Set fso = CreateObject("Scripting.FileSystemObject")
Dim shorty
On error Resume Next
shorty = fso.GetFolder(Path).ShortPath
If err.Number <> 0 then
err.Clear
Exit Sub
End IF


set obj = GetObject("Winmgmts:\\.\" & nspace).Get(classname)

Set txtstream = fso.OpenTextFile(Shorty & "\" & Classname & ".xml", 2, true, -
2)
    txtstream.WriteLine("<data>")
```

```
txtstream.WriteLine(" <NamespaceInformation>")
txtstream.WriteLine("  <namespace>" & nspace & "</namespace>")
txtstream.WriteLine("  <classname>" & classname & "</classname>")
txtstream.WriteLine(" </NamespaceInformation>")
txtstream.WriteLine(" <properties>")

for each prop in obj.Properties_
    txtstream.WriteLine("      <property Name = """ & prop.Name & """
IsArray="""    &    prop.IsArray    &    """    DataType    =    """    &
prop.Qualifiers_("CIMType").Value & """/>")
    Next
txtstream.WriteLine(" </properties>")
txtstream.WriteLine("</data>")
txtstream.close

End sub
```

As shown below, once these routines are done, you should be able to go to the folder, based on what I've told you about the Namespace\category\classes

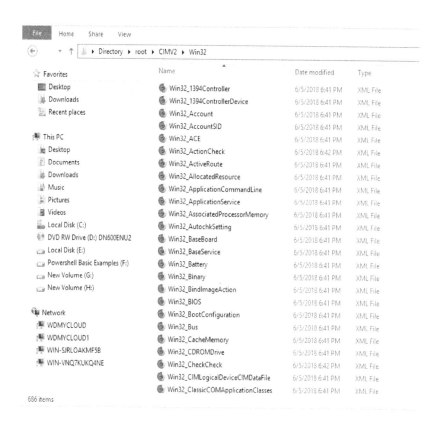

And If you open one of these up:

```xml
- <data>
  - <NamespaceInformation>
      <namespace>root\CIMV2</namespace>
      <classname>Win32_BIOS</classname>
    </NamespaceInformation>
  - <properties>
      <property Name="BiosCharacteristics" IsArray="True" DataType="uint16"/>
      <property Name="BIOSVersion" IsArray="True" DataType="string"/>
      <property Name="BuildNumber" IsArray="False" DataType="string"/>
      <property Name="Caption" IsArray="False" DataType="string"/>
      <property Name="CodeSet" IsArray="False" DataType="string"/>
      <property Name="CurrentLanguage" IsArray="False" DataType="string"/>
      <property Name="Description" IsArray="False" DataType="string"/>
      <property Name="IdentificationCode" IsArray="False" DataType="string"/>
      <property Name="InstallableLanguages" IsArray="False" DataType="uint16"/>
      <property Name="InstallDate" IsArray="False" DataType="datetime"/>
      <property Name="LanguageEdition" IsArray="False" DataType="string"/>
      <property Name="ListOfLanguages" IsArray="True" DataType="string"/>
      <property Name="Manufacturer" IsArray="False" DataType="string"/>
      <property Name="Name" IsArray="False" DataType="string"/>
      <property Name="OtherTargetOS" IsArray="False" DataType="string"/>
      <property Name="PrimaryBIOS" IsArray="False" DataType="boolean"/>
      <property Name="ReleaseDate" IsArray="False" DataType="datetime"/>
      <property Name="SerialNumber" IsArray="False" DataType="string"/>
      <property Name="SMBIOSBIOSVersion" IsArray="False" DataType="string"/>
      <property Name="SMBIOSMajorVersion" IsArray="False" DataType="uint16"/>
      <property Name="SMBIOSMinorVersion" IsArray="False" DataType="uint16"/>
      <property Name="SMBIOSPresent" IsArray="False" DataType="boolean"/>
      <property Name="SoftwareElementID" IsArray="False" DataType="string"/>
      <property Name="SoftwareElementState" IsArray="False" DataType="uint16"/>
      <property Name="Status" IsArray="False" DataType="string"/>
      <property Name="TargetOperatingSystem" IsArray="False" DataType="uint16"/>
      <property Name="Version" IsArray="False" DataType="string"/>
    </properties>
  </data>
```

THE MANY WAYS TO USE YOUR WMI SKILLS AND IMPRESS PEOPLE

I have a confession to make. Get-CIMInstancedoes not play fare. Allow me to explain. $objs = Get-CIMInstance-namespace root\cimv2 -class Win32_Process returns a collection of objects which can be enumerated.

On the other hand, $objs = Get-CIMInstance-namespace root\cimv2 -class Win32_Bios returns a single object.

Because of this fact, the code here assumes that the class you will be calling has a collection. Otherwise, the entire book would have to be doubled in size.

Below is the code that you could use to get around this issue should you decide later to use it.

```
$ws = New-object -com WScript.Shell
$fso = New-object -com Scripting.FileSystemObject
$txtstream          =          $fso.OpenTextFile($ws.CurrentDirectory          .
"\\Win32_Process.html", 2, $true, -2)


$objs = Get-CIMInstance-namespace root\cimv2 -class Win32_Process
$txtstream.WriteLine(html>")
$txtstream.WriteLine("<head>")
$txtstream.WriteLine("<style type='text/css'>")
$txtstream.WriteLine("body")
$txtstream.WriteLine("{")
$txtstream.WriteLine("    PADDING-RIGHT: 0px;")
$txtstream.WriteLine("    PADDING-LEFT: 0px;")
$txtstream.WriteLine("    PADDING-BOTTOM: 0px;")
```

```
$txtstream.WriteLine("    MARGIN: 0px;")
$txtstream.WriteLine("    COLOR: #333;")
$txtstream.WriteLine("    PADDING-TOP: 0px;")
$txtstream.WriteLine("        FONT-FAMILY: verdana, arial, helvetica, sans-
serif;")
$txtstream.WriteLine("}")
$txtstream.WriteLine("table")
$txtstream.WriteLine("{")
$txtstream.WriteLine("    BORDER-RIGHT: #999999 1px solid;")
$txtstream.WriteLine("    PADDING-RIGHT: 1px;")
$txtstream.WriteLine("    PADDING-LEFT: 1px;")
$txtstream.WriteLine("    PADDING-BOTTOM: 1px;")
$txtstream.WriteLine("    LINE-HEIGHT: 8px;")
$txtstream.WriteLine("    PADDING-TOP: 1px;")
$txtstream.WriteLine("    BORDER-BOTTOM: #999 1px solid;")
$txtstream.WriteLine("    BACKGROUND-COLOR: #eeeeee;")
$txtstream.WriteLine("
filter:progid:DXImageTransform.Microsoft.Shadow(color='silver',    Direction=135,
Strength=16)")
$txtstream.WriteLine("}")
$txtstream.WriteLine("th")
$txtstream.WriteLine("{")
$txtstream.WriteLine("    BORDER-RIGHT: #999999 3px solid;")
$txtstream.WriteLine("    PADDING-RIGHT: 6px;")
$txtstream.WriteLine("    PADDING-LEFT: 6px;")
$txtstream.WriteLine("    FONT-WEIGHT: Bold;")
$txtstream.WriteLine("    FONT-SIZE: 14px;")
$txtstream.WriteLine("    PADDING-BOTTOM: 6px;")
$txtstream.WriteLine("    COLOR: darkred;")
$txtstream.WriteLine("    LINE-HEIGHT: 14px;")
$txtstream.WriteLine("    PADDING-TOP: 6px;")
$txtstream.WriteLine("    BORDER-BOTTOM: #999 1px solid;")
$txtstream.WriteLine("    BACKGROUND-COLOR: #eeeeee;")
```

```
$txtstream.WriteLine("   FONT-FAMILY: font-family: Cambria, serif;")
$txtstream.WriteLine("   FONT-SIZE: 12px;")
$txtstream.WriteLine("   text-align: left;")
$txtstream.WriteLine("   white-Space: nowrap;")
$txtstream.WriteLine("}")
$txtstream.WriteLine(".th")
$txtstream.WriteLine("{")
$txtstream.WriteLine("   BORDER-RIGHT: #999999 2px solid;")
$txtstream.WriteLine("   PADDING-RIGHT: 6px;")
$txtstream.WriteLine("   PADDING-LEFT: 6px;")
$txtstream.WriteLine("   FONT-WEIGHT: Bold;")
$txtstream.WriteLine("   PADDING-BOTTOM: 6px;")
$txtstream.WriteLine("   COLOR: black;")
$txtstream.WriteLine("   PADDING-TOP: 6px;")
$txtstream.WriteLine("   BORDER-BOTTOM: #999 2px solid;")
$txtstream.WriteLine("   BACKGROUND-COLOR: #eeeeee;")
$txtstream.WriteLine("   FONT-FAMILY: font-family: Cambria, serif;")
$txtstream.WriteLine("   FONT-SIZE: 10px;")
$txtstream.WriteLine("   text-align: right;")
$txtstream.WriteLine("   white-Space: nowrap;")
$txtstream.WriteLine("}")
$txtstream.WriteLine("td")
$txtstream.WriteLine("{")
$txtstream.WriteLine("   BORDER-RIGHT: #999999 3px solid;")
$txtstream.WriteLine("   PADDING-RIGHT: 6px;")
$txtstream.WriteLine("   PADDING-LEFT: 6px;")
$txtstream.WriteLine("   FONT-WEIGHT: Normal;")
$txtstream.WriteLine("   PADDING-BOTTOM: 6px;")
$txtstream.WriteLine("   COLOR: navy;")
$txtstream.WriteLine("   LINE-HEIGHT: 14px;")
$txtstream.WriteLine("   PADDING-TOP: 6px;")
$txtstream.WriteLine("   BORDER-BOTTOM: #999 1px solid;")
$txtstream.WriteLine("   BACKGROUND-COLOR: #eeeeee;")
```

```
$txtstream.WriteLine("    FONT-FAMILY: font-family: Cambria, serif;")
$txtstream.WriteLine("    FONT-SIZE: 12px;")
$txtstream.WriteLine("    text-align: left;")
$txtstream.WriteLine("    white-Space: nowrap;")
$txtstream.WriteLine("}")
$txtstream.WriteLine("div")
$txtstream.WriteLine("{")
$txtstream.WriteLine("    BORDER-RIGHT: #999999 3px solid;")
$txtstream.WriteLine("    PADDING-RIGHT: 6px;")
$txtstream.WriteLine("    PADDING-LEFT: 6px;")
$txtstream.WriteLine("    FONT-WEIGHT: Normal;")
$txtstream.WriteLine("    PADDING-BOTTOM: 6px;")
$txtstream.WriteLine("    COLOR: white;")
$txtstream.WriteLine("    PADDING-TOP: 6px;")
$txtstream.WriteLine("    BORDER-BOTTOM: #999 1px solid;")
$txtstream.WriteLine("    BACKGROUND-COLOR: navy;")
$txtstream.WriteLine("    FONT-FAMILY: font-family: Cambria, serif;")
$txtstream.WriteLine("    FONT-SIZE: 10px;")
$txtstream.WriteLine("    text-align: left;")
$txtstream.WriteLine("    white-Space: nowrap;")
$txtstream.WriteLine("}")
$txtstream.WriteLine("span")
$txtstream.WriteLine("{")
$txtstream.WriteLine("    BORDER-RIGHT: #999999 3px solid;")
$txtstream.WriteLine("    PADDING-RIGHT: 3px;")
$txtstream.WriteLine("    PADDING-LEFT: 3px;")
$txtstream.WriteLine("    FONT-WEIGHT: Normal;")
$txtstream.WriteLine("    PADDING-BOTTOM: 3px;")
$txtstream.WriteLine("    COLOR: white;")
$txtstream.WriteLine("    PADDING-TOP: 3px;")
$txtstream.WriteLine("    BORDER-BOTTOM: #999 1px solid;")
$txtstream.WriteLine("    BACKGROUND-COLOR: navy;")
$txtstream.WriteLine("    FONT-FAMILY: font-family: Cambria, serif;")
```

```
$txtstream.WriteLine("   FONT-SIZE: 10px;")
$txtstream.WriteLine("   text-align: left;")
$txtstream.WriteLine("   white-Space: nowrap;")
$txtstream.WriteLine("   display: inline-block;")
$txtstream.WriteLine("   width: 100%;")
$txtstream.WriteLine("}")
$txtstream.WriteLine("textarea")
$txtstream.WriteLine("{")
$txtstream.WriteLine("   BORDER-RIGHT: #999999 3px solid;")
$txtstream.WriteLine("   PADDING-RIGHT: 3px;")
$txtstream.WriteLine("   PADDING-LEFT: 3px;")
$txtstream.WriteLine("   FONT-WEIGHT: Normal;")
$txtstream.WriteLine("   PADDING-BOTTOM: 3px;")
$txtstream.WriteLine("   COLOR: white;")
$txtstream.WriteLine("   PADDING-TOP: 3px;")
$txtstream.WriteLine("   BORDER-BOTTOM: #999 1px solid;")
$txtstream.WriteLine("   BACKGROUND-COLOR: navy;")
$txtstream.WriteLine("   FONT-FAMILY: font-family: Cambria, serif;")
$txtstream.WriteLine("   FONT-SIZE: 10px;")
$txtstream.WriteLine("   text-align: left;")
$txtstream.WriteLine("   white-Space: nowrap;")
$txtstream.WriteLine("   width: 100%;")
$txtstream.WriteLine("}")
$txtstream.WriteLine("select")
$txtstream.WriteLine("{")
$txtstream.WriteLine("   BORDER-RIGHT: #999999 3px solid;")
$txtstream.WriteLine("   PADDING-RIGHT: 6px;")
$txtstream.WriteLine("   PADDING-LEFT: 6px;")
$txtstream.WriteLine("   FONT-WEIGHT: Normal;")
$txtstream.WriteLine("   PADDING-BOTTOM: 6px;")
$txtstream.WriteLine("   COLOR: white;")
$txtstream.WriteLine("   PADDING-TOP: 6px;")
$txtstream.WriteLine("   BORDER-BOTTOM: #999 1px solid;")
```

```
$txtstream.WriteLine("    BACKGROUND-COLOR: navy;")
$txtstream.WriteLine("    FONT-FAMILY: font-family: Cambria, serif;")
$txtstream.WriteLine("    FONT-SIZE: 10px;")
$txtstream.WriteLine("    text-align: left;")
$txtstream.WriteLine("    white-Space: nowrap;")
$txtstream.WriteLine("    width: 100%;")
$txtstream.WriteLine("}")
$txtstream.WriteLine("input")
$txtstream.WriteLine("{")
$txtstream.WriteLine("    BORDER-RIGHT: #999999 3px solid;")
$txtstream.WriteLine("    PADDING-RIGHT: 3px;")
$txtstream.WriteLine("    PADDING-LEFT: 3px;")
$txtstream.WriteLine("    FONT-WEIGHT: Bold;")
$txtstream.WriteLine("    PADDING-BOTTOM: 3px;")
$txtstream.WriteLine("    COLOR: white;")
$txtstream.WriteLine("    PADDING-TOP: 3px;")
$txtstream.WriteLine("    BORDER-BOTTOM: #999 1px solid;")
$txtstream.WriteLine("    BACKGROUND-COLOR: navy;")
$txtstream.WriteLine("    FONT-FAMILY: font-family: Cambria, serif;")
$txtstream.WriteLine("    FONT-SIZE: 12px;")
$txtstream.WriteLine("    text-align: left;")
$txtstream.WriteLine("    display: table-cell;")
$txtstream.WriteLine("    white-Space: nowrap;")
$txtstream.WriteLine("    width: 100%;")
$txtstream.WriteLine("}")
$txtstream.WriteLine("h1 {")
$txtstream.WriteLine("color: antiquewhite;")
$txtstream.WriteLine("text-shadow: 1px 1px 1px black;")
$txtstream.WriteLine("padding: 3px;")
$txtstream.WriteLine("text-align: center;")
$txtstream.WriteLine("box-shadow: inset 2px 2px 5px rgba(0,0,0,0.5), inset -
2px -2px 5px rgba(255,255,255,0.5)")
$txtstream.WriteLine("}")
```

```
$txtstream.WriteLine("</style>")
$txtstream.WriteLine("<title>Win32_Process</title>")
$txtstream.WriteLine("</head>")
$txtstream.WriteLine("<body>")
$txtstream.WriteLine("<table Border='1' cellpadding='1' cellspacing='1'>")
    if($objs.Count -eq $null)
    {
  $txtstream.WriteLine("<tr>")
foreach($prop in $objs.Properties)
{
    $txtstream.WriteLine("<th>" + $prop.Name + "</th>)")
}
$txtstream.WriteLine("</tr>")
      $txtstream.WriteLine("<tr>")
  foreach($prop in $objs.Properties)
  {
    $txtstream.WriteLine("<td>" + GetValue($prop.Name, $objs) + "</td>)")
      }
  $txtstream.WriteLine("</tr>")
   }
   else
   {
  $obj = $objs.ItemIndex(0)
  $txtstream.WriteLine("<tr>")
  foreach($prop in $obj.Properties)
  {
    $txtstream.WriteLine("<th>" + $prop.Name + "</th>)")
      }
  $txtstream.WriteLine("</tr>")
  foreach($obj in $objs)
  {
    $txtstream.WriteLine("<tr>")
  foreach($prop in $obj.Properties)
```

```
    {
        $txtstream.WriteLine("<td>" + GetValue($prop.Name, $obj) + "</td>)")
    }
    $txtstream.WriteLine("</tr>")
  }
}
$txtstream.WriteLine("</table>")
$txtstream.WriteLine("</body>")
$txtstream.WriteLine("</html>")
$txtstream.Close()
```

As you can see from this, you can pretty much imagine how much more pages would have to be added to this book just to include examples for both ways.

The following is list of the what we're going to be using with WMI:

ASP
ASPX
Attribute XML
Delimited Files
Element XML
Element XML For XSL
Excel
HTA
HTML
Schema XML
XSL

I need to do this before someone complains.

Up to here, the various languages I'm going to cover will have the same chapters. But past here, the code is specifically for each language. All will have the same code examples but written in the language specified in the title.

WORKING WITH ASP

The concept of programs writing programs

I NEED TO SHARE SOMETHING IMPOTANT WITH YOU THAT I HAVE SEEN ASKED BY PROS OVER AND OVER AGAIN. THE FACT THAT THEY ARE ASKING IT SHOWS JUST HOW UNAWARE THEY ARE OF THIS IMPORTANT FACT. Anything you write inside a textstream is considered by the compiler to be a string and not code.

So, if I type:

For VBScript, VB, VBS, VB.Net, Python, Ruby:
$txtstream.WriteLine("Response.Write(""<tr>"" & vbcrlf) ")
For JavaScript, JScript:
$txtstream.WriteLine("Response.Write(""<tr>"" & vbcrlf) ")
For Kixtart:
$txtstream.WriteLine("Response.Write(""<tr>"" & vbcrlf) ")
For C#:
$txtstream.WriteLine("Response.Write(\"<tr>\" & vbcrlf) ")
For C. . :
txtstream.WriteLine("Response.Write(\"<tr>\" & vbcrlf) ")
For PowerShell:
$txtstream.WriteLine("Response.Write(""<tr>"" & vbcrlf) ")
For Rexx:
txtstream~WriteLine("Response.Write(""<tr>"" & vbcrlf) ")

For Borland C Builder:

```
txtstream.OLEFunction("WriteLine",   OleVariant("Response.Write(""""<tr>""""   &
vbcrlf) ")
```

For Borland Delphi:

```
$txtstream.WriteLine('Response.Write("<tr> '' & vbcrlf) ')
```

Aside from conforming to the compiler's expectations for single and double quotes, see any difference in the Response.Write("<tr>" & vbcrlf). It's because that part of the code is written to run as VBScript.

That also means any of the 14 languages listed could also create any of the other 14 languages. Hence, Programs that write programs. Below, is the code for ASP. The getValue function is in Appendix B.

```
$objs = Get-CIMInstance-namespace root\cimv2 -class Win32_Process

$ws = New-object -com WScript.Shell

$txtstream          =          $fso.OpenTextFile($ws.CurrentDirectory         .
"\\Win32_Process.asp", 2, $true, -2)
```

For Single Line Horizontal

```
$txtstream.WriteLine("<html>")
$txtstream.WriteLine("<head>")
$txtstream.WriteLine("<style type='text/css'>")
$txtstream.WriteLine("th")
$txtstream.WriteLine("{")
$txtstream.WriteLine("    COLOR: darkred;")
$txtstream.WriteLine("    BACKGROUND-COLOR: white;")
$txtstream.WriteLine("    FONT-FAMILY:font-family: Cambria, serif;")
$txtstream.WriteLine("    FONT-SIZE: 12px;")
$txtstream.WriteLine("    text-align: left;")
$txtstream.WriteLine("    white-Space: nowrap;")
$txtstream.WriteLine("}")
$txtstream.WriteLine("td")
```

```
$txtstream.WriteLine("{")
$txtstream.WriteLine("    COLOR: navy;")
$txtstream.WriteLine("    BACKGROUND-COLOR: white;")
$txtstream.WriteLine("    FONT-FAMILY: font-family: Cambria, serif;")
$txtstream.WriteLine("    FONT-SIZE: 12px;")
$txtstream.WriteLine("    text-align: left;")
$txtstream.WriteLine("    white-Space: nowrap;")
$txtstream.WriteLine("}")
$txtstream.WriteLine("</style>")
$txtstream.WriteLine("<title>Win32_Process</title>")
$txtstream.WriteLine("</head>")
$txtstream.WriteLine("<body>")
```

Use this if you want to create a border around your table:
```
$txtstream.WriteLine("<table Border='1' cellpadding='1' cellspacing='1'>")
```

Use this if you don't want to create a border around your table:
```
$txtstream.WriteLine("<table Border='0' cellpadding='1' cellspacing='1'>")
```

```
$txtstream.WriteLine("<%")
$obj = $objs.ItemIndex(0)
$txtstream.WriteLine("Response.Write(""<tr>"" & vbcrlf)")
foreach($prop in $obj.Properties)
{
    $txtstream.WriteLine("Response.Write(""<th>" + $prop.Name + "</th>"" & vbcrlf)")
}
$txtstream.WriteLine("Response.Write(""</tr>"" & vbcrlf)")
$txtstream.WriteLine("Response.Write(""<tr>"" & vbcrlf)")

foreach($prop in $obj.Properties)
{
```

```
$txtstream.WriteLine("Response.Write(""<td>"   +   GetValue($prop.Name,
$obj) + "</td>""" & vbcrlf)")
    }
$txtstream.WriteLine("Response.Write(""</tr>""" & vbcrlf)")
$txtstream.WriteLine("%>")
$txtstream.WriteLine("</table>")
$txtstream.WriteLine("</body>")
$txtstream.WriteLine("</html>")
$txtstream.Close()
```

For Multi Line Horizontal

```
$txtstream.WriteLine("<html>")
$txtstream.WriteLine("<head>")
$txtstream.WriteLine("<style type='text/css'>")
$txtstream.WriteLine("th")
$txtstream.WriteLine("{")
$txtstream.WriteLine("   COLOR: darkred;")
$txtstream.WriteLine("   BACKGROUND-COLOR: white;")
$txtstream.WriteLine("   FONT-FAMILY:font-family: Cambria, serif;")
$txtstream.WriteLine("   FONT-SIZE: 12px;")
$txtstream.WriteLine("   text-align: left;")
$txtstream.WriteLine("   white-Space: nowrap;")
$txtstream.WriteLine("}")
$txtstream.WriteLine("td")
$txtstream.WriteLine("{")
$txtstream.WriteLine("   COLOR: navy;")
$txtstream.WriteLine("   BACKGROUND-COLOR: white;")
$txtstream.WriteLine("   FONT-FAMILY: font-family: Cambria, serif;")
$txtstream.WriteLine("   FONT-SIZE: 12px;")
$txtstream.WriteLine("   text-align: left;")
$txtstream.WriteLine("   white-Space: nowrap;")
$txtstream.WriteLine("}")
```

```
$txtstream.WriteLine("</style>")
$txtstream.WriteLine("<title>Win32_Process</title>")
$txtstream.WriteLine("</head>")
$txtstream.WriteLine("<body>")
```

Use this if you want to create a border around your table:
```
$txtstream.WriteLine("<table Border='1' cellpadding='1' cellspacing='1'>")
```

Use this if you don't want to create a border around your table:
```
$txtstream.WriteLine("<table Border='0' cellpadding='1' cellspacing='1'>")
```

```
$txtstream.WriteLine("<%")
$obj = $objs.ItemIndex(0)
$txtstream.WriteLine("Response.Write(""<tr>"" & vbcrlf)")
foreach($prop in $obj.Properties)
{
    $txtstream.WriteLine("Response.Write(""<th>" + $prop.Name + "</th>"" &
vbcrlf)")
}
$txtstream.WriteLine("Response.Write(""</tr>"" & vbcrlf)")
foreach($obj in $objs)
{
    $txtstream.WriteLine("Response.Write(""<tr>"" & vbcrlf)")
    foreach($prop in $obj.Properties)
    {
        $txtstream.WriteLine("Response.Write(""<td>" + GetValue($prop.Name,
$obj) + "</td>"" & vbcrlf)")
    }
    $txtstream.WriteLine("Response.Write(""</tr>"" & vbcrlf)")
}
$txtstream.WriteLine("%>")
$txtstream.WriteLine("</table>")
$txtstream.WriteLine("</body>")
```

```
$txtstream.WriteLine("</html>")
$txtstream.Close()
```

For Single Line Vertical

```
$txtstream.WriteLine("<html>")
$txtstream.WriteLine("<head>")
$txtstream.WriteLine("<style type='text/css'>")
$txtstream.WriteLine("th")
$txtstream.WriteLine("{")
$txtstream.WriteLine("   COLOR: darkred;")
$txtstream.WriteLine("   BACKGROUND-COLOR: white;")
$txtstream.WriteLine("   FONT-FAMILY:font-family: Cambria, serif;")
$txtstream.WriteLine("   FONT-SIZE: 12px;")
$txtstream.WriteLine("   text-align: left;")
$txtstream.WriteLine("   white-Space: nowrap;")
$txtstream.WriteLine("}")
$txtstream.WriteLine("td")
$txtstream.WriteLine("{")
$txtstream.WriteLine("   COLOR: navy;")
$txtstream.WriteLine("   BACKGROUND-COLOR: white;")
$txtstream.WriteLine("   FONT-FAMILY: font-family: Cambria, serif;")
$txtstream.WriteLine("   FONT-SIZE: 12px;")
$txtstream.WriteLine("   text-align: left;")
$txtstream.WriteLine("   white-Space: nowrap;")
$txtstream.WriteLine("}")
$txtstream.WriteLine("</style>")
$txtstream.WriteLine("<title>Win32_Process</title>")
$txtstream.WriteLine("</head>")
$txtstream.WriteLine("<body>")
```

Use this if you want to create a border around your table:
```
$txtstream.WriteLine("<table Border='1' cellpadding='1' cellspacing='1'>")
```

Use this if you don't want to create a border around your table:

```
$txtstream.WriteLine("<table Border='0' cellpadding='1' cellspacing='1'>")


$txtstream.WriteLine("<%>")
$obj = $objs.ItemIndex(0)
foreach($prop in $obj.Properties)
{
    $txtstream.WriteLine("Response.Write(""<tr><th>"    +    $prop.Name    +
"</th>(""""<td>" + GetValue($prop.Name, $obj) + "</td></tr>""" & vbcrlf)")
}
$txtstream.WriteLine("%>")
$txtstream.WriteLine("</table>")
$txtstream.WriteLine("</body>")
$txtstream.WriteLine("</html>")
$txtstream.Close()
```

For Multi Line Vertical

```
$txtstream.WriteLine("<html>")
$txtstream.WriteLine("<head>")
$txtstream.WriteLine("<style type='text/css'>")
$txtstream.WriteLine("th")
$txtstream.WriteLine("{")
$txtstream.WriteLine("    COLOR: darkred;")
$txtstream.WriteLine("    BACKGROUND-COLOR: white;")
$txtstream.WriteLine("    FONT-FAMILY:font-family: Cambria, serif;")
$txtstream.WriteLine("    FONT-SIZE: 12px;")
$txtstream.WriteLine("    text-align: left;")
$txtstream.WriteLine("    white-Space: nowrap;")
$txtstream.WriteLine("}")
$txtstream.WriteLine("td")
$txtstream.WriteLine("{")
$txtstream.WriteLine("    COLOR: navy;")
```

```
$txtstream.WriteLine("    BACKGROUND-COLOR: white;")
$txtstream.WriteLine("    FONT-FAMILY: font-family: Cambria, serif;")
$txtstream.WriteLine("    FONT-SIZE: 12px;")
$txtstream.WriteLine("    text-align: left;")
$txtstream.WriteLine("    white-Space: nowrap;")
$txtstream.WriteLine("}")
$txtstream.WriteLine("</style>")
$txtstream.WriteLine("<title>Win32_Process</title>")
$txtstream.WriteLine("</head>")
$txtstream.WriteLine("<body>")
```

Use this if you want to create a border around your table:
```
$txtstream.WriteLine("<table Border='1' cellpadding='1' cellspacing='1'>")
```

Use this if you don't want to create a border around your table:
```
$txtstream.WriteLine("<table Border='0' cellpadding='1' cellspacing='1'>")
$txtstream.WriteLine("<%")
$obj = $objs.ItemIndex(0)
foreach($prop in $obj.Properties)
{
    $txtstream.WriteLine("Response.Write(""<tr><th>"    +    $prop.Name    +
"</th>"" & vbcrlf)")
        foreach($obj1 in $objs)
        {
            $txtstream.WriteLine("Response.Write(""<td>"  +  GetValue($prop.Name,
$obj1) + "</td>"" & vbcrlf)")
        }
        $txtstream.WriteLine("Response.Write(""</tr>"" & vbcrlf)")
    }
    $txtstream.WriteLine("%>")
    $txtstream.WriteLine("</table>")
    $txtstream.WriteLine("</body>")
    $txtstream.WriteLine("</html>")
```

```
$txtstream.Close()
```

ASPX CODE

Below, is the code for ASP. The getValue function is in Appendix B.

$objs = Get-CIMInstance-namespace root\cimv2 –class Win32_Process

$ws = New-object -com WScript.Shell
$txtstream = $fso.OpenTextFile($ws.CurrentDirectory + "\Win32_Process.aspx", 2, $true, -2)

For Single Line Horizontal

```
$txtstream.WriteLine("<!DOCTYPE html PUBLIC ""-//W3C//DTD XHTML 1.0 Transitional//EN"" ""http://www.w3.org/TR/xhtml1/DTD/xhtml1-transitional.dtd"">")
$txtstream.WriteLine("")
$txtstream.WriteLine("<html xmlns="http://www.w3.org/1999/xhtml" >")
$txtstream.WriteLine("<head>")
$txtstream.WriteLine("<style type='text/css'>")
$txtstream.WriteLine("th")
$txtstream.WriteLine("{")
$txtstream.WriteLine("   COLOR: darkred;")
$txtstream.WriteLine("   BACKGROUND-COLOR: white;")
$txtstream.WriteLine("   FONT-FAMILY:font-family: Cambria, serif;")
$txtstream.WriteLine("   FONT-SIZE: 12px;")
$txtstream.WriteLine("   text-align: left;")
$txtstream.WriteLine("   white-Space: nowrap;")
$txtstream.WriteLine("}")
$txtstream.WriteLine("td")
$txtstream.WriteLine("{")
```

```
$txtstream.WriteLine("   COLOR: navy;")
$txtstream.WriteLine("   BACKGROUND-COLOR: white;")
$txtstream.WriteLine("   FONT-FAMILY: font-family: Cambria, serif;")
$txtstream.WriteLine("   FONT-SIZE: 12px;")
$txtstream.WriteLine("   text-align: left;")
$txtstream.WriteLine("   white-Space: nowrap;")
$txtstream.WriteLine("}")
$txtstream.WriteLine("</style>")
$txtstream.WriteLine("<title>Win32_Process</title>")
$txtstream.WriteLine("</head>")
$txtstream.WriteLine("<body>")
```

Use this if you want to create a border around your table:

```
$txtstream.WriteLine("<table Border='1' cellpadding='1' cellspacing='1'>")
```

Use this if you don't want to create a border around your table:

```
$txtstream.WriteLine("<table Border='0' cellpadding='1' cellspacing='1'>")
$txtstream.WriteLine("<%")
$obj = $objs.ItemIndex(0)
$txtstream.WriteLine("Response.Write(""<tr>"" & vbcrlf)")
foreach($prop in $obj.Properties)
{
    $txtstream.WriteLine("Response.Write(""<th>" + $prop.Name + "</th>"" & vbcrlf)")
}
$txtstream.WriteLine("Response.Write(""</tr>"" & vbcrlf)")
$txtstream.WriteLine("Response.Write(""<tr>"" & vbcrlf)")
foreach($prop in $obj.Properties)
{
    $txtstream.WriteLine("Response.Write(""<td>"   +   GetValue($prop.Name, $obj) + "</td>"" & vbcrlf)")
}
$txtstream.WriteLine("Response.Write(""</tr>"" & vbcrlf)")
```

```
$txtstream.WriteLine("%>")
$txtstream.WriteLine("</table>")
$txtstream.WriteLine("</body>")
$txtstream.WriteLine("</html>")
$txtstream.Close()
```

For Multi Line Horizontal

```
    $txtstream.WriteLine("<!DOCTYPE html PUBLIC ""-//W3C//DTD XHTML
1.0        Transitional//EN""        ""http://www.w3.org/TR/xhtml1/DTD/xhtml1-
transitional.dtd"">")
    $txtstream.WriteLine("")
        $txtstream.WriteLine("<html
xmlns="http://www.w3.org/1999/xhtml"
    >")
    $txtstream.WriteLine("<head>")
    $txtstream.WriteLine("<style type='text/css'>")
    $txtstream.WriteLine("th")
    $txtstream.WriteLine("{")
    $txtstream.WriteLine("    COLOR: darkred;")
    $txtstream.WriteLine("    BACKGROUND-COLOR: white;")
    $txtstream.WriteLine("    FONT-FAMILY:font-family: Cambria, serif;")
    $txtstream.WriteLine("    FONT-SIZE: 12px;")
    $txtstream.WriteLine("    text-align: left;")
    $txtstream.WriteLine("    white-Space: nowrap;")
    $txtstream.WriteLine("}")
    $txtstream.WriteLine("td")
    $txtstream.WriteLine("{")
    $txtstream.WriteLine("    COLOR: navy;")
    $txtstream.WriteLine("    BACKGROUND-COLOR: white;")
    $txtstream.WriteLine("    FONT-FAMILY: font-family: Cambria, serif;")
    $txtstream.WriteLine("    FONT-SIZE: 12px;")
    $txtstream.WriteLine("    text-align: left;")
```

```
$txtstream.WriteLine("   white-Space: nowrap;")
$txtstream.WriteLine("}")
$txtstream.WriteLine("</style>")
$txtstream.WriteLine("<title>Win32_Process</title>")
$txtstream.WriteLine("</head>")
$txtstream.WriteLine("<body>")
```

Use this if you want to create a border around your table:
```
$txtstream.WriteLine("<table Border='1' cellpadding='1' cellspacing='1'>")
```

Use this if you don't want to create a border around your table:
```
$txtstream.WriteLine("<table Border='0' cellpadding='1' cellspacing='1'>")
```

```
$txtstream.WriteLine("<%")
$obj = $objs.ItemIndex(0)
$txtstream.WriteLine("Response.Write(""<tr>"" & vbcrlf)")
foreach($prop in $obj.Properties)
{
    $txtstream.WriteLine("Response.Write(""<th>" + $prop.Name + "</th>"" &
vbcrlf)")
}
$txtstream.WriteLine("Response.Write(""</tr>"" & vbcrlf)")
foreach($obj in $objs)
{
    $txtstream.WriteLine("Response.Write(""<tr>"" & vbcrlf)")
    foreach($prop in $obj.Properties)
    {
        $txtstream.WriteLine("Response.Write(""<td>" + GetValue($prop.Name,
$obj) + "</td>"" & vbcrlf)")
    }
    $txtstream.WriteLine("Response.Write(""</tr>"" & vbcrlf)")
}
$txtstream.WriteLine("%>")
```

```
$txtstream.WriteLine("</table>")
$txtstream.WriteLine("</body>")
$txtstream.WriteLine("</html>")
$txtstream.Close()
```

For Single Line Vertical

```
$txtstream.WriteLine("<!DOCTYPE html PUBLIC ""-//W3C//DTD XHTML
1.0      Transitional//EN""      ""http://www.w3.org/TR/xhtml1/DTD/xhtml1-
transitional.dtd"">")
$txtstream.WriteLine("")
$txtstream.WriteLine("<html
xmlns="http://www.w3.org/1999/xhtml"
>")
$txtstream.WriteLine("<head>")
$txtstream.WriteLine("<style type='text/css'>")
$txtstream.WriteLine("th")
$txtstream.WriteLine("{")
$txtstream.WriteLine("   COLOR: darkred;")
$txtstream.WriteLine("   BACKGROUND-COLOR: white;")
$txtstream.WriteLine("   FONT-FAMILY:font-family: Cambria, serif;")
$txtstream.WriteLine("   FONT-SIZE: 12px;")
$txtstream.WriteLine("   text-align: left;")
$txtstream.WriteLine("   white-Space: nowrap;")
$txtstream.WriteLine("}")
$txtstream.WriteLine("td")
$txtstream.WriteLine("{")
$txtstream.WriteLine("   COLOR: navy;")
$txtstream.WriteLine("   BACKGROUND-COLOR: white;")
$txtstream.WriteLine("   FONT-FAMILY: font-family: Cambria, serif;")
$txtstream.WriteLine("   FONT-SIZE: 12px;")
$txtstream.WriteLine("   text-align: left;")
$txtstream.WriteLine("   white-Space: nowrap;")
$txtstream.WriteLine("}")
```

```
$txtstream.WriteLine("</style>")
$txtstream.WriteLine("<title>Win32_Process</title>")
$txtstream.WriteLine("</head>")
$txtstream.WriteLine("<body>")
```

Use this if you want to create a border around your table:
```
$txtstream.WriteLine("<table Border='1' cellpadding='1' cellspacing='1'>")
```

Use this if you don't want to create a border around your table:
```
$txtstream.WriteLine("<table Border='0' cellpadding='1' cellspacing='1'>")
```

```
$txtstream.WriteLine("<%")
$obj = $objs.ItemIndex(0)
foreach($prop in $obj.Properties)
{
    $txtstream.WriteLine("Response.Write(""<tr><th>"     +     $prop.Name     +
"</th>(""""<td>" + GetValue($prop.Name, $obj) + "</td></tr>""" & vbcrlf)")
}
$txtstream.WriteLine("%>")
$txtstream.WriteLine("</table>")
$txtstream.WriteLine("</body>")
$txtstream.WriteLine("</html>")
$txtstream.Close()
```

For Multi Line Vertical

```
        $txtstream.WriteLine("<!DOCTYPE html PUBLIC ""-//W3C//DTD XHTML
1.0        Transitional//EN""        ""http://www.w3.org/TR/xhtml1/DTD/xhtml1-
transitional.dtd"">")
    $txtstream.WriteLine("")
        $txtstream.WriteLine("<html
xmlns="http://www.w3.org/1999/xhtml"
    >")
```

```
$txtstream.WriteLine("<head>")
$txtstream.WriteLine("<style type='text/css'>")
$txtstream.WriteLine("th")
$txtstream.WriteLine("{")
$txtstream.WriteLine("    COLOR: darkred;")
$txtstream.WriteLine("    BACKGROUND-COLOR: white;")
$txtstream.WriteLine("    FONT-FAMILY:font-family: Cambria, serif;")
$txtstream.WriteLine("    FONT-SIZE: 12px;")
$txtstream.WriteLine("    text-align: left;")
$txtstream.WriteLine("    white-Space: nowrap;")
$txtstream.WriteLine("}")
$txtstream.WriteLine("td")
$txtstream.WriteLine("{")
$txtstream.WriteLine("    COLOR: navy;")
$txtstream.WriteLine("    BACKGROUND-COLOR: white;")
$txtstream.WriteLine("    FONT-FAMILY: font-family: Cambria, serif;")
$txtstream.WriteLine("    FONT-SIZE: 12px;")
$txtstream.WriteLine("    text-align: left;")
$txtstream.WriteLine("    white-Space: nowrap;")
$txtstream.WriteLine("}")
$txtstream.WriteLine("</style>")
$txtstream.WriteLine("<title>Win32_Process</title>")
$txtstream.WriteLine("</head>")
$txtstream.WriteLine("<body>")
```

Use this if you want to create a border around your table:
```
$txtstream.WriteLine("<table Border='1' cellpadding='1' cellspacing='1'>")
```

Use this if you don't want to create a border around your table:
```
$txtstream.WriteLine("<table Border='0' cellpadding='1' cellspacing='1'>")
```

```
$txtstream.WriteLine("<%")
$obj = $objs.ItemIndex(0)
```

```
foreach($prop in $obj.Properties)
{
    $txtstream.WriteLine("Response.Write(""<tr><th>"   +   $prop.Name   +
"</th>""" & vbcrlf)")
    foreach($obj1 in $objs)
    {
        $txtstream.WriteLine("Response.Write(""<td>"  +  GetValue($prop.Name,
$obj1) + "</td>""" $  vbcrlf)")
    }
    $txtstream.WriteLine("Response.Write(""</tr>""" & vbcrlf)")
}
$txtstream.WriteLine("%>")
$txtstream.WriteLine("</table>")
$txtstream.WriteLine("</body>")
$txtstream.WriteLine("</html>")
$txtstream.Close()
```

HTA CODE

Below, is the code for HTA. The getValue function is in Appendix B.

$objs = Get-CIMInstance-namespace root\cimv2 –class Win32_Process

$ws = New-object -com WScript.Shell
$txtstream   = $fso.OpenTextFile($ws.CurrentDirectory   +
"\\Win32_Process.html", 2, $true, -2)

For Single Line Horizontal

```
$txtstream.WriteLine("<html>")
$txtstream.WriteLine("<head>")
$txtstream.WriteLine("<HTA:APPLICATION ")
$txtstream.WriteLine("ID = ""Process"" ")
$txtstream.WriteLine("APPLICATIONNAME = ""Process"" ")
$txtstream.WriteLine("SCROLL = ""yes"" ")
$txtstream.WriteLine("SINGLEINSTANCE = ""yes"" ")
$txtstream.WriteLine("WINDOWSTATE = ""maximize"" >")
$txtstream.WriteLine("<style type='text/css'>")
$txtstream.WriteLine("th")
$txtstream.WriteLine("{")
$txtstream.WriteLine("   COLOR: darkred;")
$txtstream.WriteLine("   BACKGROUND-COLOR: white;")
$txtstream.WriteLine("   FONT-FAMILY:font-family: Cambria, serif;")
$txtstream.WriteLine("   FONT-SIZE: 12px;")
$txtstream.WriteLine("   text-align: left;")
$txtstream.WriteLine("   white-Space: nowrap;")
$txtstream.WriteLine("}")
```

```
$txtstream.WriteLine("td")
$txtstream.WriteLine("{")
$txtstream.WriteLine("    COLOR: navy;")
$txtstream.WriteLine("    BACKGROUND-COLOR: white;")
$txtstream.WriteLine("    FONT-FAMILY: font-family: Cambria, serif;")
$txtstream.WriteLine("    FONT-SIZE: 12px;")
$txtstream.WriteLine("    text-align: left;")
$txtstream.WriteLine("    white-Space: nowrap;")
$txtstream.WriteLine("}")
$txtstream.WriteLine("</style>")
$txtstream.WriteLine("<title>Win32_Process</title>")
$txtstream.WriteLine("</head>")
$txtstream.WriteLine("<body>")
```

Use this if you want to create a border around your table:
```
$txtstream.WriteLine("<table Border='1' cellpadding='1' cellspacing='1'>")
```

Use this if you don't want to create a border around your table:
```
$txtstream.WriteLine("<table Border='0' cellpadding='1' cellspacing='1'>")
$obj = $objs.ItemIndex(0)
$txtstream.WriteLine("<tr>")
foreach($prop in $obj.Properties)
    $txtstream.WriteLine("<th>" + $prop.Name + "</th>)")
next
$txtstream.WriteLine("</tr>")
$txtstream.WriteLine("<tr>")
foreach($prop in $obj.Properties)
    $txtstream.WriteLine("<td>" + GetValue($prop.Name, $obj) + "</td>)")
next
$txtstream.WriteLine("</tr>")
$txtstream.WriteLine("</table>")
$txtstream.WriteLine("</body>")
$txtstream.WriteLine("</html>")
```

```
$txtstream.Close()
```

For Multi Line Horizontal

```
    $txtstream.WriteLine(html>")
$txtstream.WriteLine("<head>")
$txtstream.WriteLine("<HTA:APPLICATION ")
$txtstream.WriteLine("ID = ""Process"" ")
$txtstream.WriteLine("APPLICATIONNAME = ""Process"" ")
$txtstream.WriteLine("SCROLL = ""yes"" ")
$txtstream.WriteLine("SINGLEINSTANCE = ""yes"" ")
$txtstream.WriteLine("WINDOWSTATE = ""maximize"" >")
$txtstream.WriteLine("<style type='text/css'>")
$txtstream.WriteLine("th")
$txtstream.WriteLine("{")
$txtstream.WriteLine("    COLOR: darkred;")
$txtstream.WriteLine("    BACKGROUND-COLOR: white;")
$txtstream.WriteLine("    FONT-FAMILY:font-family: Cambria, serif;")
$txtstream.WriteLine("    FONT-SIZE: 12px;")
$txtstream.WriteLine("    text-align: left;")
$txtstream.WriteLine("    white-Space: nowrap;")
$txtstream.WriteLine("}")
$txtstream.WriteLine("td")
$txtstream.WriteLine("{")
$txtstream.WriteLine("    COLOR: navy;")
$txtstream.WriteLine("    BACKGROUND-COLOR: white;")
$txtstream.WriteLine("    FONT-FAMILY: font-family: Cambria, serif;")
$txtstream.WriteLine("    FONT-SIZE: 12px;")
$txtstream.WriteLine("    text-align: left;")
$txtstream.WriteLine("    white-Space: nowrap;")
$txtstream.WriteLine("}")
$txtstream.WriteLine("</style>")
$txtstream.WriteLine("<title>Win32_Process</title>")
```

```
$txtstream.WriteLine("</head>")
$txtstream.WriteLine("<body>")
```

Use this if you want to create a border around your table:
```
$txtstream.WriteLine("<table Border='1' cellpadding='1' cellspacing='1'>")
```

Use this if you don't want to create a border around your table:
```
$txtstream.WriteLine("<table Border='0' cellpadding='1' cellspacing='1'>")
```

```
$obj = $objs.ItemIndex(0)
$txtstream.WriteLine("<tr>")
foreach($prop in $obj.Properties)
{
    $txtstream.WriteLine("<th>" + $prop.Name + "</th>)")
        }
$txtstream.WriteLine("</tr>")
foreach($obj in $objs)
{
    $txtstream.WriteLine("<tr>")
    foreach($prop in $obj.Properties)
    {
        $txtstream.WriteLine("<td>" + GetValue($prop.Name, $obj) + "</td>)")
    }
    $txtstream.WriteLine("</tr>")
}
$txtstream.WriteLine("</table>")
$txtstream.WriteLine("</body>")
$txtstream.WriteLine("</html>")
$txtstream.Close()
```

For Single Line Vertical

```
$txtstream.WriteLine("<html>")
$txtstream.WriteLine("<head>")
$txtstream.WriteLine("<HTA:APPLICATION ")
$txtstream.WriteLine("ID = ""Process"" ")
$txtstream.WriteLine("APPLICATIONNAME = ""Process"" ")
$txtstream.WriteLine("SCROLL = ""yes"" ")
$txtstream.WriteLine("SINGLEINSTANCE = ""yes"" ")
$txtstream.WriteLine("WINDOWSTATE = ""maximize"" >")
$txtstream.WriteLine("<style type='text/css'>")
$txtstream.WriteLine("th")
$txtstream.WriteLine("{")
$txtstream.WriteLine("    COLOR: darkred;")
$txtstream.WriteLine("    BACKGROUND-COLOR: white;")
$txtstream.WriteLine("    FONT-FAMILY:font-family: Cambria, serif;")
$txtstream.WriteLine("    FONT-SIZE: 12px;")
$txtstream.WriteLine("    text-align: left;")
$txtstream.WriteLine("    white-Space: nowrap;")
$txtstream.WriteLine("}")
$txtstream.WriteLine("td")
$txtstream.WriteLine("{")
$txtstream.WriteLine("    COLOR: navy;")
$txtstream.WriteLine("    BACKGROUND-COLOR: white;")
$txtstream.WriteLine("    FONT-FAMILY: font-family: Cambria, serif;")
$txtstream.WriteLine("    FONT-SIZE: 12px;")
$txtstream.WriteLine("    text-align: left;")
$txtstream.WriteLine("    white-Space: nowrap;")
$txtstream.WriteLine("}")
$txtstream.WriteLine("</style>")
$txtstream.WriteLine("<title>Win32_Process</title>")
$txtstream.WriteLine("</head>")
$txtstream.WriteLine("<body>")
```

Use this if you want to create a border around your table:

```
$txtstream.WriteLine("<table Border='1' cellpadding='1' cellspacing='1'>")
```

Use this if you don't want to create a border around your table:
```
$txtstream.WriteLine("<table Border='0' cellpadding='1' cellspacing='1'>")

$obj = $objs.ItemIndex(0)
foreach($prop in $obj.Properties)
{
    $txtstream.WriteLine("<tr><th>" + $prop.Name + "</th>(""<td>" +
GetValue($prop.Name, $obj) + "</td></tr>)")
}
$txtstream.WriteLine("</table>")
$txtstream.WriteLine("</body>")
$txtstream.WriteLine("</html>")
$txtstream.Close()
```

For Multi Line Vertical

```
$txtstream.WriteLine("<html>")
$txtstream.WriteLine("<head>")
$txtstream.WriteLine("<HTA:APPLICATION ")
$txtstream.WriteLine("ID = ""Process"" ")
$txtstream.WriteLine("APPLICATIONNAME = ""Process"" ")
$txtstream.WriteLine("SCROLL = ""yes"" ")
$txtstream.WriteLine("SINGLEINSTANCE = ""yes"" ")
$txtstream.WriteLine("WINDOWSTATE = ""maximize"" >")

$txtstream.WriteLine("<style type='text/css'>")
$txtstream.WriteLine("th")
$txtstream.WriteLine("{")
$txtstream.WriteLine("    COLOR: darkred;")
$txtstream.WriteLine("    BACKGROUND-COLOR: white;")
$txtstream.WriteLine("    FONT-FAMILY:font-family: Cambria, serif;")
```

```
$txtstream.WriteLine("    FONT-SIZE: 12px;")
$txtstream.WriteLine("    text-align: left;")
$txtstream.WriteLine("    white-Space: nowrap;")
$txtstream.WriteLine("}")
$txtstream.WriteLine("td")
$txtstream.WriteLine("{")
$txtstream.WriteLine("    COLOR: navy;")
$txtstream.WriteLine("    BACKGROUND-COLOR: white;")
$txtstream.WriteLine("    FONT-FAMILY: font-family: Cambria, serif;")
$txtstream.WriteLine("    FONT-SIZE: 12px;")
$txtstream.WriteLine("    text-align: left;")
$txtstream.WriteLine("    white-Space: nowrap;")
$txtstream.WriteLine("}")
$txtstream.WriteLine("</style>")
$txtstream.WriteLine("<title>Win32_Process</title>")
$txtstream.WriteLine("</head>")
$txtstream.WriteLine("<body>")
```

Use this if you want to create a border around your table:

```
$txtstream.WriteLine("<table Border='1' cellpadding='1' cellspacing='1'>")
```

Use this if you don't want to create a border around your table:

```
$txtstream.WriteLine("<table Border='0' cellpadding='1' cellspacing='1'>")
```

```
$obj = $objs.ItemIndex(0)
foreach($prop in $obj.Properties)
{
    $txtstream.WriteLine("<tr><th>" + $prop.Name + "</th>)")
    foreach($obj1 in $objs)
    {
        $txtstream.WriteLine("<td>" + GetValue($prop.Name, $obj1)  + "</td>)")
    }
    $txtstream.WriteLine("</tr>")
```

```
}
$txtstream.WriteLine("</table>")
$txtstream.WriteLine("</body>")
$txtstream.WriteLine("</html>")
$txtstream.Close()
```

HTML CODE

Below, is the code for HTML. The getValue function is in Appendix B.

$objs = Get-CIMInstance-namespace root\cimv2 -class Win32_Process

$ws = New-object -com WScript.Shell

$txtstream   = $fso.OpenTextFile($ws.CurrentDirectory   +
"\\Win32_Process.html", 2, $true, -2)

For Single Line Horizontal

```
$txtstream.WriteLine("<html>")
$txtstream.WriteLine("<head>")
$txtstream.WriteLine("<style type='text/css'>")
$txtstream.WriteLine("th")
$txtstream.WriteLine("{")
$txtstream.WriteLine("   COLOR: darkred;")
$txtstream.WriteLine("   BACKGROUND-COLOR: white;")
$txtstream.WriteLine("   FONT-FAMILY:font-family: Cambria, serif;")
$txtstream.WriteLine("   FONT-SIZE: 12px;")
$txtstream.WriteLine("   text-align: left;")
$txtstream.WriteLine("   white-Space: nowrap;")
$txtstream.WriteLine("}")
$txtstream.WriteLine("td")
$txtstream.WriteLine("{")
$txtstream.WriteLine("   COLOR: navy;")
$txtstream.WriteLine("   BACKGROUND-COLOR: white;")
$txtstream.WriteLine("   FONT-FAMILY: font-family: Cambria, serif;")
$txtstream.WriteLine("   FONT-SIZE: 12px;")
$txtstream.WriteLine("   text-align: left;")
```

```
$txtstream.WriteLine("   white-Space: nowrap;")
$txtstream.WriteLine("}")
$txtstream.WriteLine("</style>")
$txtstream.WriteLine("<title>Win32_Process</title>")
$txtstream.WriteLine("</head>")
$txtstream.WriteLine("<body>")
```

Use this if you want to create a border around your table:
```
$txtstream.WriteLine("<table Border='1' cellpadding='1' cellspacing='1'>")
```

Use this if you don't want to create a border around your table:
```
$txtstream.WriteLine("<table Border='0' cellpadding='1' cellspacing='1'>")
$obj = $objs.ItemIndex(0)
$txtstream.WriteLine("<tr>")
foreach($prop in $obj.Properties)
    $txtstream.WriteLine("<th>" + $prop.Name + "</th>)")
next
$txtstream.WriteLine("</tr>")
$txtstream.WriteLine("<tr>")
foreach($prop in $obj.Properties)
    $txtstream.WriteLine("<td>" + GetValue($prop.Name, $obj) + "</td>)")
next
$txtstream.WriteLine("</tr>")
$txtstream.WriteLine("</table>")
$txtstream.WriteLine("</body>")
$txtstream.WriteLine("</html>")
$txtstream.Close()
```

For Multi Line Horizontal

```
$txtstream.WriteLine(html>")
$txtstream.WriteLine("<head>")
$txtstream.WriteLine("<style type='text/css'>")
```

```
$txtstream.WriteLine("th")
$txtstream.WriteLine("{")
$txtstream.WriteLine("   COLOR: darkred;")
$txtstream.WriteLine("   BACKGROUND-COLOR: white;")
$txtstream.WriteLine("   FONT-FAMILY:font-family: Cambria, serif;")
$txtstream.WriteLine("   FONT-SIZE: 12px;")
$txtstream.WriteLine("   text-align: left;")
$txtstream.WriteLine("   white-Space: nowrap;")
$txtstream.WriteLine("}")
$txtstream.WriteLine("td")
$txtstream.WriteLine("{")
$txtstream.WriteLine("   COLOR: navy;")
$txtstream.WriteLine("   BACKGROUND-COLOR: white;")
$txtstream.WriteLine("   FONT-FAMILY: font-family: Cambria, serif;")
$txtstream.WriteLine("   FONT-SIZE: 12px;")
$txtstream.WriteLine("   text-align: left;")
$txtstream.WriteLine("   white-Space: nowrap;")
$txtstream.WriteLine("}")
$txtstream.WriteLine("</style>")
$txtstream.WriteLine("<title>Win32_Process</title>")
$txtstream.WriteLine("</head>")
$txtstream.WriteLine("<body>")
```

Use this if you want to create a border around your table:

```
$txtstream.WriteLine("<table Border='1' cellpadding='1' cellspacing='1'>")
```

Use this if you don't want to create a border around your table:

```
$txtstream.WriteLine("<table Border='0' cellpadding='1' cellspacing='1'>")
```

```
$obj = $objs.ItemIndex(0)
$txtstream.WriteLine("<tr>")
foreach($prop in $obj.Properties)
{
```

```
    $txtstream.WriteLine("<th>" + $prop.Name + "</th>)")
        }
$txtstream.WriteLine("</tr>")
foreach($obj in $objs)
{
    $txtstream.WriteLine("<tr>")
    foreach($prop in $obj.Properties)
    {
        $txtstream.WriteLine("<td>" + GetValue($prop.Name, $obj) + "</td>)")
    }
    $txtstream.WriteLine("</tr>")
}
$txtstream.WriteLine("</table>")
$txtstream.WriteLine("</body>")
$txtstream.WriteLine("</html>")
$txtstream.Close()
```

For Single Line Vertical

```
    $txtstream.WriteLine("<html>")
$txtstream.WriteLine("<head>")
$txtstream.WriteLine("<style type='text/css'>")
$txtstream.WriteLine("th")
$txtstream.WriteLine("{")
$txtstream.WriteLine("   COLOR: darkred;")
$txtstream.WriteLine("   BACKGROUND-COLOR: white;")
$txtstream.WriteLine("   FONT-FAMILY:font-family: Cambria, serif;")
$txtstream.WriteLine("   FONT-SIZE: 12px;")
$txtstream.WriteLine("   text-align: left;")
$txtstream.WriteLine("   white-Space: nowrap;")
$txtstream.WriteLine("}")
$txtstream.WriteLine("td")
```

```
$txtstream.WriteLine("{")
$txtstream.WriteLine("    COLOR: navy;")
$txtstream.WriteLine("    BACKGROUND-COLOR: white;")
$txtstream.WriteLine("    FONT-FAMILY: font-family: Cambria, serif;")
$txtstream.WriteLine("    FONT-SIZE: 12px;")
$txtstream.WriteLine("    text-align: left;")
$txtstream.WriteLine("    white-Space: nowrap;")
$txtstream.WriteLine("}")
$txtstream.WriteLine("</style>")
$txtstream.WriteLine("<title>Win32_Process</title>")
$txtstream.WriteLine("</head>")
$txtstream.WriteLine("<body>")
```

Use this if you want to create a border around your table:
```
$txtstream.WriteLine("<table Border='1' cellpadding='1' cellspacing='1'>")
```

Use this if you don't want to create a border around your table:
```
$txtstream.WriteLine("<table Border='0' cellpadding='1' cellspacing='1'>")
```

```
$obj = $objs.ItemIndex(0)
foreach($prop in $obj.Properties)
{
    $txtstream.WriteLine("<tr><th>" + $prop.Name + "</th>(""<td>" +
GetValue($prop.Name, $obj) + "</td></tr>)")
}
$txtstream.WriteLine("</table>")
$txtstream.WriteLine("</body>")
$txtstream.WriteLine("</html>")
$txtstream.Close()
```
For Multi Line Vertical
```
$txtstream.WriteLine("<html>")
$txtstream.WriteLine("<head>")
$txtstream.WriteLine("<style type='text/css'>")
```

```
$txtstream.WriteLine("th")
$txtstream.WriteLine("{")
$txtstream.WriteLine("    COLOR: darkred;")
$txtstream.WriteLine("    BACKGROUND-COLOR: white;")
$txtstream.WriteLine("    FONT-FAMILY:font-family: Cambria, serif;")
$txtstream.WriteLine("    FONT-SIZE: 12px;")
$txtstream.WriteLine("    text-align: left;")
$txtstream.WriteLine("    white-Space: nowrap;")
$txtstream.WriteLine("}")
$txtstream.WriteLine("td")
$txtstream.WriteLine("{")
$txtstream.WriteLine("    COLOR: navy;")
$txtstream.WriteLine("    BACKGROUND-COLOR: white;")
$txtstream.WriteLine("    FONT-FAMILY: font-family: Cambria, serif;")
$txtstream.WriteLine("    FONT-SIZE: 12px;")
$txtstream.WriteLine("    text-align: left;")
$txtstream.WriteLine("    white-Space: nowrap;")
$txtstream.WriteLine("}")
$txtstream.WriteLine("</style>")
$txtstream.WriteLine("<title>Win32_Process</title>")
$txtstream.WriteLine("</head>")
$txtstream.WriteLine("<body>")
```

Use this if you want to create a border around your table:
```
$txtstream.WriteLine("<table Border='1' cellpadding='1' cellspacing='1'>")
```

Use this if you don't want to create a border around your table:
```
$txtstream.WriteLine("<table Border='0' cellpadding='1' cellspacing='1'>")
```

```
$obj = $objs.ItemIndex(0)
foreach($prop in $obj.Properties)
{
    $txtstream.WriteLine("<tr><th>" + $prop.Name + "</th>)")
```

```
    foreach($obj1 in $objs)
    {
        $txtstream.WriteLine("<td>" + GetValue($prop.Name, $obj1)  +  "</td>)")
    }
    $txtstream.WriteLine("</tr>")
}
$txtstream.WriteLine("</table>")
$txtstream.WriteLine("</body>")
$txtstream.WriteLine("</html>")
$txtstream.Close()
```

TEXT DELIMITED FILE EXAMPLES

Text files can be databases, too

Below, are code samples for creating various types of delimited files. The getValue function is in Appendix B.

```
$objs = Get-CIMInstance-namespace root\cimv2 -class Win32_Process
```

Colon Delimited

```
$tempstr = ""
$ws = New-object -com WScript.Shell
Set fso = CreateObject("Scripting.FileSystemObject
$txtstream         =         $fso.OpenTextFile($ws.CurrentDirectory         +
"\\Win32_Process.txt" , 2, $true, -2)
```

HORIZONTAL

```
$obj = $objs.ItemIndex(0)
Foreach($prop in $obj.Properties)
{
   if($tempstr <> "")
   {
      $tempstr = $tempstr +  "~";
   }
   $tempstr = $tempstr +  $prop.Name;
}
```

```
$txtstream.WriteLine($tempstr)
$tempstr = "";
foreach($obj in $objs)
{
    Foreach($prop in $obj.Properties)
    {
        if($tempstr ne "")
        {
            $tempstr = $tempstr  +  "~";
        }
        $tempstr = $tempstr + "" + GetValue($prop.Name, $obj) + "";
    }
    $txtstream.WriteLine($tempstr)
    $tempstr = "";
}
$txtstream.Close()
```

VERTICAL

```
$obj = $objs.ItemIndex(0)
Foreach($prop in $obj.Properties)
{
    $tempstr = $prop.Name;
    Foreach($obj in $objs)
    {
        if($tempstr ne "")
        {
        $tempstr = $tempstr  +  "~";
        }
        $tempstr = $tempstr + "" + GetValue($prop.Name, $obj) + "";
    }
    $txtstream.WriteLine($tempstr)
    $tempstr = "";
```

```
    }
    $txtstream.Close()
```

Comma Delimited

```
$tempstr = ""
$ws = New-object -com WScript.Shell
Set fso = CreateObject("Scripting.FileSystemObject
$txtstream        =        $fso.OpenTextFile($ws.CurrentDirectory        +
"\Win32_Process.csv" , 2, $true, -2)
```

```
$obj = $objs.ItemIndex(0)
Foreach($prop in $obj.Properties)
{
    if($tempstr <> "")
    {
        $tempstr = $tempstr + ",";
    }
    $tempstr = $tempstr + $prop.Name;
}
$txtstream.WriteLine($tempstr)
$tempstr = "";
foreach($obj in $objs)
{
    Foreach($prop in $obj.Properties)
    {
        if($tempstr ne "")
        {
            $tempstr = $tempstr + ",";
```

```
      }
      $tempstr = $tempstr + '''' + GetValue($prop.Name, $obj) + '''';
   }
   $txtstream.WriteLine($tempstr)
   $tempstr = "";
}
$txtstream.Close()
```

```
$obj = $objs.ItemIndex(0)
Foreach($prop in $obj.Properties)
{
   $tempstr = $prop.Name;
   Foreach($obj in $objs)
   {
      if($tempstr ne "")
      {
      $tempstr = $tempstr + ",";
      }
      $tempstr = $tempstr + '''' + GetValue($prop.Name, $obj) + '''';
   }
   $txtstream.WriteLine($tempstr)
   $tempstr = "";
}
$txtstream.Close()
```

Exclamation

```
$tempstr = ""
$ws = New-object -com WScript.Shell
Set fso = CreateObject("Scripting.FileSystemObject
```

```
$txtstream        =        $fso.OpenTextFile($ws.CurrentDirectory        +
"\\Win32_Process.txt", 2, $true, -2)
```

HORIZONTAL

```
$obj = $objs.ItemIndex(0)
Foreach($prop in $obj.Properties)
{
   if($tempstr <> """")
   {
      $tempstr = $tempstr +  "!";
   }
   $tempstr = $tempstr +  $prop.Name;
}
$txtstream.WriteLine($tempstr)
$tempstr = "";
foreach($obj in $objs)
{
   Foreach($prop in $obj.Properties)
   {
      if($tempstr ne "")
      {
         $tempstr = $tempstr  +  "!";
      }
      $tempstr = $tempstr + "" + GetValue($prop.Name, $obj) + "";
   }
   $txtstream.WriteLine($tempstr)
   $tempstr = "";
}
$txtstream.Close()
```

VERTICAL

```
$obj = $objs.ItemIndex(0)
Foreach($prop in $obj.Properties)
{
   $tempstr = $prop.Name;
   Foreach($obj in $objs)
   {
      if($tempstr ne "")
      {
      $tempstr = $tempstr + "!";
      }
      $tempstr = $tempstr + ""' + GetValue($prop.Name, $obj) + "";
   }
   $txtstream.WriteLine($tempstr)
   $tempstr = "";
}
$txtstream.Close()
```

SEMI COLON

```
$tempstr = ""
$ws = New-object -com WScript.Shell
Set fso = CreateObject("Scripting.FileSystemObject
$txtstream          =          $fso.OpenTextFile($ws.CurrentDirectory          +
"\\Win32_Process.txt", 2, $true, -2)
```

HORIZONTAL

```
$obj = $objs.ItemIndex(0)
Foreach($prop in $obj.Properties)
{
```

```
    if($tempstr <> "")
    {
       $tempstr = $tempstr +  ";";
    }
    $tempstr = $tempstr +  $prop.Name;
}
$txtstream.WriteLine($tempstr)
$tempstr = "";
foreach($obj in $objs)
{
   Foreach($prop in $obj.Properties)
   {
      if($tempstr ne "")
      {
         $tempstr = $tempstr  + ";";
      }
      $tempstr = $tempstr + "" + GetValue($prop.Name, $obj) + "";
   }
   $txtstream.WriteLine($tempstr)
   $tempstr = "";
}
$txtstream.Close()
```

VERTICAL

```
$obj = $objs.ItemIndex(0)
Foreach($prop in $obj.Properties)
{
   $tempstr = $prop.Name;
   Foreach($obj in $objs)
   {
      if($tempstr ne "")
      {
```

```
        $tempstr = $tempstr  +  ";";
        }
        $tempstr = $tempstr +  "" + GetValue($prop.Name, $obj) + "";
    }
    $txtstream.WriteLine($tempstr)
    $tempstr = "";
}
$txtstream.Close()
```

Tab Delimited

```
$tempstr = ""
$ws = New-object -com WScript.Shell
Set fso = CreateObject("Scripting.FileSystemObject
$txtstream        =        $fso.OpenTextFile($ws.CurrentDirectory        +
"\Win32_Process.txt", 2, $true, -2)
```

HORIZONTAL

```
$obj = $objs.ItemIndex(0)
Foreach($prop in $obj.Properties)
{
    if($tempstr <> "")
    {
        $tempstr = $tempstr +  "\t";
    }
    $tempstr = $tempstr +  $prop.Name;
}
$txtstream.WriteLine($tempstr)
```

```
$tempstr = "";
foreach($obj in $objs)
{
   Foreach($prop in $obj.Properties)
   {
      if($tempstr ne "")
      {
         $tempstr = $tempstr  + "\t";
      }
      $tempstr = $tempstr + "" + GetValue($prop.Name, $obj) + "";
   }
   $txtstream.WriteLine($tempstr)
   $tempstr = "";
}
```

VERTICAL

```
$obj = $objs.ItemIndex(0)
Foreach($prop in $obj.Properties)
{
   $tempstr = $prop.Name;
   Foreach($obj in $objs)
   {
      if($tempstr ne "")
      {
      $tempstr = $tempstr  + "\t";
      }
      $tempstr = $tempstr + "" + GetValue($prop.Name, $obj) + ""
   }
   $txtstream.WriteLine($tempstr)
   $tempstr = "";
}
```

```
$txtstream.Close()
```

Tilde Delimited

```
$tempstr = "";
$ws = New-object -com WScript.Shell
Set fso = CreateObject("Scripting.FileSystemObject
$txtstream       =       $fso.OpenTextFile($ws.CurrentDirectory       +
"\\Win32_Process.txt", 2, $true, -2)
```

HORIZONTAL

```
$obj = $objs.ItemIndex(0)
Foreach($prop in $obj.Properties)
{
   if($tempstr <> "")
   {
      $tempstr = $tempstr + "~";
   }
   $tempstr = $tempstr + $prop.Name;
}
$txtstream.WriteLine($tempstr)
$tempstr = "";
foreach($obj in $objs)
{
   Foreach($prop in $obj.Properties)
   {
      if($tempstr ne "")
      {
         $tempstr = $tempstr + "~";
```

```
        }
        $tempstr = $tempstr + ''' + GetValue($prop.Name, $obj) + ''';
    }
    $txtstream.WriteLine($tempstr)
    $tempstr = "";
}
$txtstream.Close()
```

VERTICAL

```
$obj = $objs.ItemIndex(0)
Foreach($prop in $obj.Properties)
{
    $tempstr = $prop.Name;
    Foreach($obj in $objs)
    {
        if($tempstr ne "")
        {
        $tempstr = $tempstr + "~";
        }
        $tempstr = $tempstr + ''' + GetValue($prop.Name, $obj) + ''';
    }
    $txtstream.WriteLine($tempstr)
    $tempstr = "";
}
$txtstream.Close()
```

THE XML FILES

Because they are out there

W

ELL, I THOUGHT IT WAS CATCHY. Below, are examples of different types of XML that can be used with the MSDAOSP and MSPERSIST Providers. Element XML as a standalone -no XSL referenced – can be used with the MSDAOSP Provider and Schema XML can be used with MSPersist.

Element XML

```
$objs = Get-CIMInstance-namespace root\cimv2 -class Win32_Process

$ws = New-object -com WScript.Shell
$txtstream        =        $fso.OpenTextFile($ws.CurrentDirectory        +
"\\Win32_Process.xml", 2, $true, -2)
$txtstream.WriteLine("<?xml version='1.0' encoding='iso-8859-1'?>")
$txtstream.WriteLine("<data>")
foreach($obj in $objs)
{
    $txtstream.WriteLine("<Win32_process>")
    foreach($prop in $obj.Properties)
    {
        $txtstream.WriteLine("<" + $prop.Name + ">" + GetValue($prop.Name,
obj). "</" + $prop.Name + ">")
```

```
    }
    $txtstream.WriteLine("</Win32_process>")
  }
  $txtstream.WriteLine("</data>")
  $txtstream.Close()
```

WMI to Element XML For XSL

```
$objs = Get-CIMInstance-namespace root\cimv2 -class Win32_Process

$ws = New-object -com WScript.Shell
$txtstream          =          $fso.OpenTextFile($ws.CurrentDirectory          +
"\\Win32_Process.xml", 2, $true, -2)
$txtstream.WriteLine("<?xml version='1.0' encoding='iso-8859-1'?>")
$txtstream.WriteLine("<?xml-stylesheet    type='Text/xsl'    href=""""    +
ws.CurrentDirectory + "\\Win32_Process.xsl"""?>")

$txtstream.WriteLine("<data>")
foreach($obj in $objs)
{
   $txtstream.WriteLine("<Win32_process>")
   foreach($prop in $obj.Properties)
   {
      $txtstream.WriteLine("<" + $prop.Name + ">" + GetValue($prop.Name,
obj). "</" + $prop.Name + ">")
   }
   $txtstream.WriteLine("</Win32_process>")
}
$txtstream.WriteLine("</data>")
$txtstream.Close()
```

SCHEMA XML

```
$objs = Get-CIMInstance-namespace root\cimv2 -class Win32_Process

$ws = New-object -com WScript.Shell
$txtstream          =          $fso.OpenTextFile($ws.CurrentDirectory          +
"\\Win32_Process.xml", 2, $true, -2)
$txtstream.WriteLine("<?xml version='1.0' encoding='iso-8859-1'?>")
$txtstream.WriteLine("<data>")
foreach($obj in $objs)
{
   $txtstream.WriteLine("<Win32_process>")
   foreach($prop in $obj.Properties)
   {
       $txtstream.WriteLine("<" + $prop.Name + ">" + GetValue($prop.Name,
obj). "</" + $prop.Name + ">")
   }
   $txtstream.WriteLine("</Win32_process>")
}
$txtstream.WriteLine("</data>")
$txtstream.Close()

$rs1 = New-object -com ("ADODB.Recordset
$rs1.ActiveConnection          =          "Provider=MSDAOSP;          Data
Source=msxml2.DSOControl"
$rs1.Open(ws.CurrentDirectory + "\\Win32_Process.xml")

if($fso.FileExists(ws.CurrentDirectory + "\\Win32_Process_Schema.xml") eq
$true)
{
   $fso.DeleteFile($ws.CurrentDirectory + "\\Win32_Process_Schema.xml")
```

```
}
$rs1..Save($ws.CurrentDirectory +  "\\Win32_Process_Schema.xml, 1) ;
```

EXCEL

Three ways to get the job done

THERE ARE THREE WAYS TO PUT DATA INTO EXCEL. CREATE A COMA DELIMITED FILE AND THEN USE WS.RUN, THROUGH AUTOMATION AND BY CREATING A PHYSICAL SPREADSHEET. Below are examples of doing exactly that.

Using the comma delimited file

```
$tempstr = "";
$ws = New-object -com WScript.Shell
$fso = New-object -com ("Scripting.FileSystemObject
$txtstream          =          $fso.OpenTextFile($ws.CurrentDirectory          +
"\\Win32_Process.csv" , 2, $true, -2)
```

HORIZONTAL

```
$obj = $objs.ItemIndex(0)
Foreach($prop in $obj.Properties)
{
    if($tempstr <> "")
    {
        $tempstr = $tempstr +  ",";
    }
    $tempstr = $tempstr +  $prop.Name;
}
$txtstream.WriteLine($tempstr)
$tempstr = "";
foreach($obj in $objs)
```

```
{
   foreach($prop in $obj.Properties)
     if($tempstr ne "")
     {
        $tempstr = $tempstr  +  ",";
     }
     $tempstr = $tempstr + "" + GetValue($prop.Name, $obj) + ""
   }
   $txtstream.WriteLine($tempstr)
   $tempstr = "";
}
$txtstream.Close()
$ws.Run($ws.CurrentDirectory +  "\\Win32_Process.csv")
```

```
$obj = $objs.ItemIndex(0)
Foreach($prop in $obj.Properties)
{
   $tempstr = $prop.Name
   Foreach($obj1 in $objs)
   {
     if($tempstr ne "")
     {
        $tempstr = $tempstr  +  ",";
     }
     $tempstr = $tempstr + "" + GetValue($prop.Name, $obj) + "";
   }
   $txtstream.WriteLine($tempstr)
   $tempstr = "";
}
$txtstream.Close()
```

```
$ws.Run($ws.CurrentDirectory +  "\\Win32_Process.csv")
```

Excel Automation

```
$objs = Get-CIMInstance-namespace root\cimv2 -class Win32_Process

$oExcel = New-object -com ("Excel.Application
$oExcel.Visible = $true;
$wb = $oExcel.Workbooks.Add()
$ws = $wb.Worksheets(0)
$ws.Name = "Win32_Process";
$y=2;
$x=1;
$obj = $objs.ItemIndex(0)
foreach($prop in $obj.Properties)
{
    $ws.Cells.Item(1, $x) = $prop.Name;
    $x=$x. 1;
}
$x=1;
foreach($obj in $objs)
{
    foreach($prop in $obj.Properties))
    {
        $ws.Cells.Item($y, $x) = GetValue($prop.Name, obj)
        $x=$x. 1;
    }
```

```
   $x=1;
   $y=$y. 1;
}
$ws.Columns.HorizontalAlignment = -4131;
$ws.Columns.AutoFit()
```

```
$objs = Get-CIMInstance-namespace root\cimv2 -class Win32_Process

$oExcel = New-object -com  ("Excel.Application
$oExcel.Visible = $true;
$wb = $oExcel.Workbooks.Add()
$ws = $wb.Worksheets(0)
$ws.Name = "Win32_Process";
$y=2;
$x=1;
$obj = $objs.ItemIndex(0)
foreach($prop in $obj.Properties)
{
   $ws.Cells.Item($x, 1) = $prop.Name;
   $x=$x. 1;
}
$x=1;
foreach($obj in $objs)
{
   foreach($prop in $obj.Properties))
   {
      $ws.Cells.Item($x, $y) = GetValue($prop.Name, obj)
      $x=$x. 1;
```

```
}
  $x=1;
  $y=$y. 1;
}
$ws.Columns.HorizontalAlignment = -4131;
$ws.Columns.AutoFit()
```

Using A Spreadsheet

```
$objs = Get-CIMInstance-namespace root\cimv2 -class Win32_Process
```

```
$ws = New-object -com WScript.Shell
$fso = New-object -com Scripting.FileSystemObject
$txtstream = $fso.OpenTextFile($ws.CurrentDirectory +  "\\ProcessExcel.xml",
2, $true, -2)
$txtstream.WriteLine("<?xml version='1.0'?>")
$txtstream.WriteLine("<?mso-application progid='Excel.Sheet'?>")
$txtstream.WriteLine("<Workbook          xmlns='urn:schemas-microsoft-
com:office:spreadsheet'        xmlns:o='urn:schemas-microsoft-com:office:office'
xmlns:x='urn:schemas-microsoft-com:office:excel'        xmlns:ss='urn:schemas-
microsoft-com:office:spreadsheet'        xmlns:html='http://www.w3.org/TR/REC-
html40'>")
$txtstream.WriteLine("          <Document$properties      xmlns='urn:schemas-
microsoft-com:office:office'>")
$txtstream.WriteLine("                    <Author>Windows User</Author>")
$txtstream.WriteLine("                    <LastAuthor>Windows
User</LastAuthor>")
$txtstream.WriteLine("                    <Created>2007-11-
27T19:36:16Z</Created>")
```

```
$txtstream.WriteLine("                    <Version>12.00</Version>")
$txtstream.WriteLine("              </Document$properties>")
$txtstream.WriteLine("        <ExcelWorkbook              xmlns='urn:schemas-microsoft-com:office:excel'>")
$txtstream.WriteLine("
   <WindowHeight>11835</WindowHeight>")
$txtstream.WriteLine("
   <WindowWidth>18960</WindowWidth>")
$txtstream.WriteLine("                    <WindowTopX>120</WindowTopX>")
$txtstream.WriteLine("                    <WindowTopY>135</WindowTopY>")
$txtstream.WriteLine("
   <ProtectStructure>False</ProtectStructure>")
$txtstream.WriteLine("
   <ProtectWindows>False</ProtectWindows>")
$txtstream.WriteLine("              </ExcelWorkbook>")
$txtstream.WriteLine("         <Styles>")
$txtstream.WriteLine("              <Style              ss:ID='Default' ss:Name='Normal'>")
$txtstream.WriteLine("                         <Alignment ss:Vertical='Bottom'/>")
$txtstream.WriteLine("                         <Borders/>")
$txtstream.WriteLine("                    <Font    ss:FontName='Calibri' x:Family='Swiss' ss:Size='11' ss:Color='#000000'/>")
$txtstream.WriteLine("                    <Interior/>")
$txtstream.WriteLine("                    <NumberFormat/>")
$txtstream.WriteLine("                    <Protection/>")
$txtstream.WriteLine("              </Style>")
$txtstream.WriteLine("              <Style ss:ID='s62'>")
$txtstream.WriteLine("                    <Borders/>")
$txtstream.WriteLine("                    <Font    ss:FontName='Calibri' x:Family='Swiss' ss:Size='11' ss:Color='#000000' ss:Bold='1'/>")
$txtstream.WriteLine("              </Style>")
$txtstream.WriteLine("              <Style ss:ID='s63'>")
```

```
$txtstream.WriteLine("                                    <Alignment
ss:Horizontal='Left' ss:Vertical='Bottom' ss:Indent='2'/>")
    $txtstream.WriteLine("                                    <Font  ss:FontName='Verdana'
x:Family='Swiss' ss:Size='7.7' ss:Color='#000000'/>")
    $txtstream.WriteLine("                </Style>")
    $txtstream.WriteLine("   </Styles>")
    $txtstream.WriteLine("<Worksheet ss:Name='Process'>")
    $txtstream.WriteLine("            <Table    x:FullColumns='1'    x:FullRows='1'
ss:DefaultRowHeight='24.9375'>")
    $txtstream.WriteLine("            <Column ss:AutoFitWidth='1' ss:Width='82.5'
ss:Span='5'/>")
    Foreach($obj in $objs)
    {
        $txtstream.WriteLine("      <Row ss:AutoFitHeight='0'>")
        Foreach($prop in $obj.Properties)
        {
            $txtstream.WriteLine("                        <Cell   ss:StyleID='s62'><Data
ss:Type='String'>" + $prop.Name + "</Data></Cell>")
        }
        $txtstream.WriteLine("      </Row>")
        Break
        }


    Foreach($obj in $objs)
    {
        $txtstream.WriteLine("      <Row ss:AutoFitHeight='0' ss:Height='13.5'>")
        foreach($prop in $obj.Properties)
        {
            $txtstream.WriteLine("        <Cell><Data ss:Type='String'><![CDATA[" +
GetValue($prop.Name, $obj) + "]]></Data></Cell>")
        }
        $txtstream.WriteLine("      </Row>")
```

```
        }
        $txtstream.WriteLine("   </Table>")
        $txtstream.WriteLine("          <WorksheetOptions          xmlns='urn:schemas-
microsoft-com:office:excel'>")
        $txtstream.WriteLine("                   <PageSetup>")
        $txtstream.WriteLine("                       <Header x:Margin='0.3'/>")
        $txtstream.WriteLine("                       <Footer x:Margin='0.3'/>")
        $txtstream.WriteLine("                       <PageMargins x:Bottom='0.75'
x:Left='0.7' x:Right='0.7' x:Top='0.75'/>")
        $txtstream.WriteLine("                   </PageSetup>")
        $txtstream.WriteLine("                   <Unsynced/>")
        $txtstream.WriteLine("              <Print>")
        $txtstream.WriteLine("                     <FitHeight>0</FitHeight>")
        $txtstream.WriteLine("                     <ValidPrinterInfo/>")
        $txtstream.WriteLine("
    <HorizontalResolution>600</HorizontalResolution>")
        $txtstream.WriteLine("
    <VerticalResolution>600</VerticalResolution>")
        $txtstream.WriteLine("              </Print>")
        $txtstream.WriteLine("              <Selected/>")
        $txtstream.WriteLine("              <Panes>")
        $txtstream.WriteLine("                     <Pane>")
        $txtstream.WriteLine("
    <Number>3</Number>")
        $txtstream.WriteLine("
    <ActiveRow>9</ActiveRow>")
        $txtstream.WriteLine("
    <ActiveCol>7</ActiveCol>")
        $txtstream.WriteLine("                     </Pane>")
        $txtstream.WriteLine("              </Panes>")
        $txtstream.WriteLine("
    <ProtectObjects>False</ProtectObjects>")
```

```
$txtstream.WriteLine("
    <ProtectScenarios>False</ProtectScenarios>")
$txtstream.WriteLine("        </WorksheetOptions>")
$txtstream.WriteLine("</Worksheet>")
$txtstream.WriteLine("</Workbook>")
$txtstream.Close()()
ws.Run(ws.CurrentDirectory + "\ProcessExcel.xml")
```

XSL

The end of the line

BELOW ARE WAYS YOU CAN CREATE XSL FILES TO RENDER YOU XML. Viewer discretion is advised.

$objs = Get-CIMInstance-namespace root\cimv2 -class Win32_Process

$ws = New-object -com WScript.Shell

$fso = New-object -com Scripting.FileSystemObject

$txtstream= $fso.OpenTextFile($ws.CurrentDirectory + "\\Process.xsl", 2, $true, -2)

SINGLE LINE HORIZONTAL

$txtstream.WriteLine("<?xml version=""1.0" " encoding=""UTF-8" "?>")

$txtstream.WriteLine("<xsl:stylesheet   version=""1.0"" xmlns:xsl=""http://www.w3.org/1999/XSL/Transform" ">")

$txtstream.WriteLine("<xsl:template match=""/"">")

$txtstream.WriteLine("<html>")

$txtstream.WriteLine("<head>")

$txtstream.WriteLine("<title>Products</title>")

$txtstream.WriteLine("<style type='text/css'>")

$txtstream.WriteLine("th")

$txtstream.WriteLine("{")

```
$txtstream.WriteLine("    COLOR: darkred;")
$txtstream.WriteLine("    BACKGROUND-COLOR: white;")
$txtstream.WriteLine("    FONT-FAMILY:font-family: Cambria, serif;")
$txtstream.WriteLine("    FONT-SIZE: 12px;")
$txtstream.WriteLine("    text-align: left;")
$txtstream.WriteLine("    white-Space: nowrap;")
$txtstream.WriteLine("}")
$txtstream.WriteLine("td")
$txtstream.WriteLine("{")
$txtstream.WriteLine("    COLOR: navy;")
$txtstream.WriteLine("    BACKGROUND-COLOR: white;")
$txtstream.WriteLine("    FONT-FAMILY: font-family: Cambria, serif;")
$txtstream.WriteLine("    FONT-SIZE: 12px;")
$txtstream.WriteLine("    text-align: left;")
$txtstream.WriteLine("    white-Space: nowrap;")
$txtstream.WriteLine("}")
$txtstream.WriteLine("</style>")
$txtstream.WriteLine("</head>")
$txtstream.WriteLine("<body bgcolor=""#333333" ">")
$txtstream.WriteLine("<table colspacing=""3" " colpadding=""3" ">")
$obj = $objs.ItemIndex(0)
$txtstream.WriteLine("<tr>")
foreach($prop in $obj.Properties)
{
    $txtstream.WriteLine("<th>" + $prop.Name + </th>")
}
$txtstream.WriteLine("</tr>")
$txtstream.WriteLine("<tr>")
foreach($prop in $obj.Properties)
{
    $txtstream.WriteLine("<td><xsl:value-of select=""data/Win32_Process/" +
$prop.Name + """/></td>")
}
```

```
$txtstream.WriteLine("</tr>")
$txtstream.WriteLine("</table>")
$txtstream.WriteLine("</body>")
$txtstream.WriteLine("</html>")
$txtstream.WriteLine("</xsl:template>")
$txtstream.WriteLine("</xsl:stylesheet>")
$txtstream.Close()()
```

For Multi Line Horizontal

```
$txtstream.WriteLine("<?xml version=""1.0" " encoding=""UTF-8" "?>")
$txtstream.WriteLine("<xsl:stylesheet                    version=""1.0""
xmlns:xsl=""http://www.w3.org/1999/XSL/Transform" ">")
$txtstream.WriteLine("<xsl:template match=""/""">")
$txtstream.WriteLine("<html>")
$txtstream.WriteLine("<head>")
$txtstream.WriteLine("<title>Products</title>")
$txtstream.WriteLine("<style type='text/css'>")
$txtstream.WriteLine("th")
$txtstream.WriteLine("{")
$txtstream.WriteLine("    COLOR: darkred;")
$txtstream.WriteLine("    BACKGROUND-COLOR: white;")
$txtstream.WriteLine("    FONT-FAMILY:font-family: Cambria, serif;")
$txtstream.WriteLine("    FONT-SIZE: 12px;")
$txtstream.WriteLine("    text-align: left;")
$txtstream.WriteLine("    white-Space: nowrap;")
$txtstream.WriteLine("}")
$txtstream.WriteLine("td")
$txtstream.WriteLine("{")
$txtstream.WriteLine("    COLOR: navy;")
$txtstream.WriteLine("    BACKGROUND-COLOR: white;")
```

```
$txtstream.WriteLine("   FONT-FAMILY: font-family: Cambria, serif;")
$txtstream.WriteLine("   FONT-SIZE: 12px;")
$txtstream.WriteLine("   text-align: left;")
$txtstream.WriteLine("   white-Space: nowrap;")
$txtstream.WriteLine("}")
$txtstream.WriteLine("</style>")
$txtstream.WriteLine("</head>")
$txtstream.WriteLine("<body bgcolor=""#333333"">")
$txtstream.WriteLine("<table colspacing=""3"" colpadding=""3"">")


$obj = $objs.ItemIndex(0)
$txtstream.WriteLine("<tr>")
foreach($prop in $obj.Properties)
{
    $txtstream.WriteLine("<th>" + $prop.Name + </th>")
}
$txtstream.WriteLine("</tr>")
$txtstream.WriteLine("<xsl:for-each select=""data/Win32_Process"">")
$txtstream.WriteLine("<tr>")
foreach($prop in $obj.Properties)
{
    $txtstream.WriteLine("<td><xsl:value-of   select=""   +   $prop.Name   +
"""/></td>")
}
$txtstream.WriteLine("</tr>")
$txtstream.WriteLine("</xsl:for-each>")
$txtstream.WriteLine("</table>")
$txtstream.WriteLine("</body>")
$txtstream.WriteLine("</html>")
$txtstream.WriteLine("</xsl:template>")
$txtstream.WriteLine("</xsl:stylesheet>")
$txtstream.Close()()
```

For Single Line Vertical

```
$txtstream.WriteLine("<?xml version=""1.0" " encoding=""UTF-8" "?>")
$txtstream.WriteLine("<xsl:stylesheet                              version=""1.0""
xmlns:xsl=""http://www.w3.org/1999/XSL/Transform" ">")
$txtstream.WriteLine("<xsl:template match=""/"">")
$txtstream.WriteLine("<html>")
$txtstream.WriteLine("<head>")
$txtstream.WriteLine("<title>Products</title>")
$txtstream.WriteLine("<style type='text/css'>")
$txtstream.WriteLine("th")
$txtstream.WriteLine("{")
$txtstream.WriteLine("   COLOR: darkred;")
$txtstream.WriteLine("   BACKGROUND-COLOR: white;")
$txtstream.WriteLine("   FONT-FAMILY:font-family: Cambria, serif;")
$txtstream.WriteLine("   FONT-SIZE: 12px;")
$txtstream.WriteLine("   text-align: left;")
$txtstream.WriteLine("   white-Space: nowrap;")
$txtstream.WriteLine("}")
$txtstream.WriteLine("td")
$txtstream.WriteLine("{")
$txtstream.WriteLine("   COLOR: navy;")
$txtstream.WriteLine("   BACKGROUND-COLOR: white;")
$txtstream.WriteLine("   FONT-FAMILY: font-family: Cambria, serif;")
$txtstream.WriteLine("   FONT-SIZE: 12px;")
$txtstream.WriteLine("   text-align: left;")
$txtstream.WriteLine("   white-Space: nowrap;")
$txtstream.WriteLine("}")
$txtstream.WriteLine("</style>")
$txtstream.WriteLine("</head>")
$txtstream.WriteLine("<body bgcolor=""#333333" ">")
```

```
$txtstream.WriteLine("<table colspacing=""3" " colpadding=""3" ">")


obj = objs.ItemIndex[0]
foreach($prop in $obj.Properties)
{
    $txtstream.WriteLine("<tr><th>" + $prop.Name + </th>")
    $txtstream.WriteLine("<td><xsl:value-of select="""data/Win32_Process/" +
$prop.Name + """/></td></tr>")
}
$txtstream.WriteLine("</table>")
$txtstream.WriteLine("</body>")
$txtstream.WriteLine("</html>")
$txtstream.WriteLine("</xsl:template>")
$txtstream.WriteLine("</xsl:stylesheet>")
$txtstream.Close()()
```

For Multi Line Vertical

```
$txtstream.WriteLine("<?xml version=""1.0" " encoding=""UTF-8" "?>")
$txtstream.WriteLine("<xsl:stylesheet                    version=""1.0""
xmlns:xsl=""http://www.w3.org/1999/XSL/Transform" ">")
$txtstream.WriteLine("<xsl:template match=""/"">")
$txtstream.WriteLine("<html>")
$txtstream.WriteLine("<head>")
$txtstream.WriteLine("<title>Products</title>")
$txtstream.WriteLine("<style type='text/css'>")
$txtstream.WriteLine("th")
```

```
$txtstream.WriteLine("{")
$txtstream.WriteLine("   COLOR: darkred;")
$txtstream.WriteLine("   BACKGROUND-COLOR: white;")
$txtstream.WriteLine("   FONT-FAMILY:font-family: Cambria, serif;")
$txtstream.WriteLine("   FONT-SIZE: 12px;")
$txtstream.WriteLine("   text-align: left;")
$txtstream.WriteLine("   white-Space: nowrap;")
$txtstream.WriteLine("}")
$txtstream.WriteLine("td")
$txtstream.WriteLine("{")
$txtstream.WriteLine("   COLOR: navy;")
$txtstream.WriteLine("   BACKGROUND-COLOR: white;")
$txtstream.WriteLine("   FONT-FAMILY: font-family: Cambria, serif;")
$txtstream.WriteLine("   FONT-SIZE: 12px;")
$txtstream.WriteLine("   text-align: left;")
$txtstream.WriteLine("   white-Space: nowrap;")
$txtstream.WriteLine("}")
$txtstream.WriteLine("</style>")
$txtstream.WriteLine("</head>")
$txtstream.WriteLine("<body bgcolor=""#333333" ">")
$txtstream.WriteLine("<table colspacing=""3" " colpadding=""3" ">")

$txtstream.WriteLine("<tr>")
obj = objs.ItemIndex[0]
foreach($prop in $obj.Properties)
   $txtstream.WriteLine("<tr><th>" + $prop.Name + </th>")
   $txtstream.WriteLine("<td><xsl:for-each
select=""data/Win32_Process"">")
   $txtstream.WriteLine("<xsl:value-of    select=""""    +    $prop.Name    +
""""/></td>")
   $txtstream.WriteLine("</xsl:for-each></tr>")
next
$txtstream.WriteLine("</table>")
```

```
$txtstream.WriteLine("</body>")
$txtstream.WriteLine("</html>")
$txtstream.WriteLine("</xsl:template>")
$txtstream.WriteLine("</xsl:stylesheet>")
$txtstream.Close()()
```

STYLESHEETS

The difference between boring and oh, wow!

The stylesheets in Appendix A, were used to render these pages. If you find one you like, feel free to use it.

Report:

Table

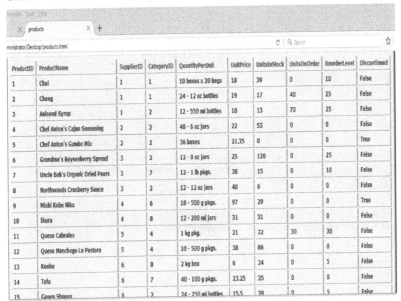

ProductID	ProductName	SupplierID	CategoryID	QuantityPerUnit	UnitPrice	UnitsInStock	UnitsOnOrder	ReorderLevel	Discontinued
1	Chai	1	1	10 boxes x 20 bags	18	39	0	10	False
2	Chang	1	1	24 - 12 oz bottles	19	17	40	25	False
3	Aniseed Syrup	1	2	12 - 550 ml bottles	10	13	70	25	False
4	Chef Anton's Cajun Seasoning	2	2	48 - 6 oz jars	22	53	0	0	False
5	Chef Anton's Gumbo Mix	2	2	36 boxes	21.35	0	0	0	True
6	Grandma's Boysenberry Spread	3	2	12 - 8 oz jars	25	120	0	25	False
7	Uncle Bob's Organic Dried Pears	3	7	12 - 1 lb pkgs.	30	15	0	10	False
8	Northwoods Cranberry Sauce	3	2	12 - 12 oz jars	40	6	0	0	False
9	Mishi Kobe Niku	4	6	18 - 500 g pkgs.	97	29	0	0	True
10	Ikura	4	8	12 - 200 ml jars	31	31	0	0	False
11	Queso Cabrales	5	4	1 kg pkg.	21	22	30	30	False
12	Queso Manchego La Pastora	5	4	10 - 500 g pkgs.	38	86	0	0	False
13	Konbu	6	8	2 kg box	6	24	0	5	False
14	Tofu	6	7	40 - 100 g pkgs.	23.25	35	0	0	False
15	Genen Shouyu	6	2	24 - 250 ml bottles	15.5	39	0	5	False

None:

Black and White

Colored:

AccountExpires	AuthorizationFlags	BadPasswordCount	Caption	CodePage	Comment	CountryCode	Description
			NT AUTHORITY\SYSTEM				Network login profile settings for SYSTEM on NT AUTHORITY
			NT AUTHORITY\LOCAL SERVICE				Network login profile settings for LOCAL SERVICE on NT AUTHORITY
			NT AUTHORITY\NETWORK SERVICE				Network login profile settings for NETWORK SERVICE on NT AUTHORITY
	0	0	Administrator	0	Built-in account for administering the computer/domain	0	Network login profile settings for on WIN-S3RLOAKMF7B
			NT SERVICE\SSASTELEMETRY				Network login profile settings for SSASTELEMETRY on NT SERVICE
			NT SERVICE\SSISTELEMETRY130				Network login profile settings for SSISTELEMETRY130 on NT SERVICE
			NT SERVICE\SQLTELEMETRY				Network login profile settings for SQLTELEMETRY on NT SERVICE
			NT SERVICE\MSSQLServerOLAPService				Network login profile settings for MSSQLServerOLAPService on NT SERVICE
			NT SERVICE\ReportServer				Network login profile settings for ReportServer on NT SERVICE
			NT SERVICE\MSSQLFDLauncher				Network login profile settings for MSSQLFDLauncher on NT SERVICE
			NT SERVICE\MSSQLLaunchpad				Network login profile settings for MSSQLLaunchpad on NT SERVICE
			NT SERVICE\MsDtsServer130				Network login profile settings for MsDtsServer130 on NT SERVICE
			NT SERVICE\MSSQLSERVER				Network login profile settings for MSSQLSERVER on NT SERVICE
			IIS APPPOOL\Classic .NET AppPool				Network login profile settings for Classic .NET AppPool on IIS APPPOOL
			IIS APPPOOL\.NET v4.5				Network login profile settings for .NET v4.5 on IIS APPPOOL
			IIS APPPOOL\.NET v2.0				Network login profile settings for .NET v2.0 on IIS APPPOOL
			IIS APPPOOL\.NET v4.5 Classic				Network login profile settings for .NET v4.5 Classic on IIS APPPOOL
			IIS APPPOOL\.NET v2.0 Classic				Network login profile settings for .NET v2.0 Classic on IIS APPPOOL

Oscillating:

Availability	BytesPerSector	Capabilities	CapabilityDescriptions	Caption	CompressionMethod	ConfigManagerErrorCode	ConfigManagerUserConfig
	512	3, 4, 10	Random Access, Supports Writing, SMART Notification	OCZ REVODRIVE350 SCSI Disk Device		0	FALSE
	512	3, 4	Random Access, Supports Writing	NVMe TOSHIBA-RD400		0	FALSE
	512	3, 4, 10	Random Access, Supports Writing, SMART Notification	TOSHIBA DT01ACA200		0	FALSE

3D:

Availability	BytesPerSector	Capabilities	CapabilityDescriptions	Caption	CompressionMethod	ConfigManagerErrorCode	ConfigManagerUserConfig	CreationClassName
	512	3, 4, 10	Random Access, Supports Writing, SMART Notification	OCZ REVODRIVE350 SCSI Disk Device		0	FALSE	Win32_DiskDrive
	512	3, 4	Random Access, Supports Writing	NVMe TOSHIBA-RD400		0	FALSE	Win32_DiskDrive
	512	3, 4, 10	Random Access, Supports Writing, SMART Notification	TOSHIBA DT01ACA200		0	FALSE	Win32_DiskDrive

Shadow Box:

Availability	BytesPerSector	Capabilities	CapabilityDescriptions	Caption	CompressionMethod	ConfigManagerErrorCode	ConfigManagerUserConfig	CreationClassName	DefaultBlockSize
	512	3, 4, 10	Random Access, Supports Writing, SMART Notification	OCZ REVODRIVE350 SCSI Disk Device		0	FALSE	Win32_DiskDrive	
	512	3, 4	Random Access, Supports Writing	NVMe TOSHIBA-RD400		0	FALSE	Win32_DiskDrive	
	512	3, 4, 10	Random Access, Supports Writing, SMART Notification	TOSHIBA DT01ACA200		0	FALSE	Win32_DiskDrive	

Shadow Box Single Line Vertical

BiosCharacteristics	7, 10, 11, 12, 15, 16, 17, 19, 23, 24, 25, 26, 27, 28, 29, 32, 33, 40, 42, 43, 48, 50, 58, 59, 64, 65, 66, 67, 68, 69, 70, 71, 72, 73, 74, 75, 76, 77, 78, 79
BIOSVersion	ALASKA - 1072009, 0504, American Megatrends - 5000C
BuildNumber	
Caption	0504
CodeSet	
CurrentLanguage	en|US|iso8859-1
Description	0504
IdentificationCode	
InstallableLanguages	8
InstallDate	
LanguageEdition	
ListOfLanguages	en|US|iso8859-1, fr|FR|iso8859-1, zh|CN|unicode,,,,,
Manufacturer	American Megatrends Inc.
Name	0504
OtherTargetOS	
PrimaryBIOS	TRUE

Shadow Box Multi line Vertical

89

Availability			
BytesPerSector	512	512	512
Capabilities	3, 4, 10	3, 4	3, 4, 10
CapabilityDescriptions	Random Access, Supports Writing, SMART Notification	Random Access, Supports Writing	Random Access, Supports Writing, SMART Notification
Caption	OCZ REVODRIVE350 SCSI Disk Device	NVMe TOSHIBA-RD400	TOSHIBA DT01ACA200
CompressionMethod			
ConfigManagerErrorCode	0	0	0
ConfigManagerUserConfig	FALSE	FALSE	FALSE
CreationClassName	Win32_DiskDrive	Win32_DiskDrive	Win32_DiskDrive
DefaultBlockSize			
Description	Disk drive	Disk drive	Disk drive
DeviceID	\\.\PHYSICALDRIVE2	\\.\PHYSICALDRIVE1	\\.\PHYSICALDRIVE0
ErrorCleared			
ErrorDescription			
ErrorMethodology			
FirmwareRevision	2.50	57CZ4102	MX6OABB0
Index	2	1	0

STYLESHEETS

Decorating your web pages

BELOW ARE SOME STYLESHEETS I COOKED UP THAT I LIKE AND THINK YOU MIGHT TOO. Don't worry I won't be offended if you take and modify to your hearts delight. Please do!

NONE

```
$txtstream.WriteLine("<style type='text/css'>")
$txtstream.WriteLine("th")
$txtstream.WriteLine("{")
$txtstream.WriteLine("   COLOR: darkred;")
$txtstream.WriteLine("}")
$txtstream.WriteLine("td")
$txtstream.WriteLine("{")
$txtstream.WriteLine("   COLOR: Navy;")
$txtstream.WriteLine("}")
$txtstream.WriteLine("</style>")
```

BLACK AND WHITE TEXT

```
$txtstream.WriteLine("<style type='text/css'>")
$txtstream.WriteLine("th")
$txtstream.WriteLine("{")
$txtstream.WriteLine("   COLOR: white;")
$txtstream.WriteLine("   BACKGROUND-COLOR: black;")
$txtstream.WriteLine("   FONT-FAMILY:font-family: Cambria, serif;")
```

```
$txtstream.WriteLine("   FONT-SIZE: 12px;")
$txtstream.WriteLine("   text-align: left;")
$txtstream.WriteLine("   white-Space: nowrap;")
$txtstream.WriteLine("}")
$txtstream.WriteLine("td")
$txtstream.WriteLine("{")
$txtstream.WriteLine("   COLOR: white;")
$txtstream.WriteLine("   BACKGROUND-COLOR: black;")
$txtstream.WriteLine("   FONT-FAMILY: font-family: Cambria, serif;")
$txtstream.WriteLine("   FONT-SIZE: 12px;")
$txtstream.WriteLine("   text-align: left;")
$txtstream.WriteLine("   white-Space: nowrap;")
$txtstream.WriteLine("}")
$txtstream.WriteLine("div")
$txtstream.WriteLine("{")
$txtstream.WriteLine("   COLOR: white;")
$txtstream.WriteLine("   BACKGROUND-COLOR: black;")
$txtstream.WriteLine("   FONT-FAMILY: font-family: Cambria, serif;")
$txtstream.WriteLine("   FONT-SIZE: 10px;")
$txtstream.WriteLine("   text-align: left;")
$txtstream.WriteLine("   white-Space: nowrap;")
$txtstream.WriteLine("}")
$txtstream.WriteLine("span")
$txtstream.WriteLine("{")
$txtstream.WriteLine("   COLOR: white;")
$txtstream.WriteLine("   BACKGROUND-COLOR: black;")
$txtstream.WriteLine("   FONT-FAMILY: font-family: Cambria, serif;")
$txtstream.WriteLine("   FONT-SIZE: 10px;")
$txtstream.WriteLine("   text-align: left;")
$txtstream.WriteLine("   white-Space: nowrap;")
$txtstream.WriteLine("   display:inline-block;")
$txtstream.WriteLine("   width: 100%;")
$txtstream.WriteLine("}")
```

```
$txtstream.WriteLine("textarea")
$txtstream.WriteLine("{")
$txtstream.WriteLine("   COLOR: white;")
$txtstream.WriteLine("   BACKGROUND-COLOR: black;")
$txtstream.WriteLine("   FONT-FAMILY: font-family: Cambria, serif;")
$txtstream.WriteLine("   FONT-SIZE: 10px;")
$txtstream.WriteLine("   text-align: left;")
$txtstream.WriteLine("   white-Space: nowrap;")
$txtstream.WriteLine("   width: 100%;")
$txtstream.WriteLine("}")
$txtstream.WriteLine("select")
$txtstream.WriteLine("{")
$txtstream.WriteLine("   COLOR: white;")
$txtstream.WriteLine("   BACKGROUND-COLOR: black;")
$txtstream.WriteLine("   FONT-FAMILY: font-family: Cambria, serif;")
$txtstream.WriteLine("   FONT-SIZE: 10px;")
$txtstream.WriteLine("   text-align: left;")
$txtstream.WriteLine("   white-Space: nowrap;")
$txtstream.WriteLine("   width: 100%;")
$txtstream.WriteLine("}")
$txtstream.WriteLine("input")
$txtstream.WriteLine("{")
$txtstream.WriteLine("   COLOR: white;")
$txtstream.WriteLine("   BACKGROUND-COLOR: black;")
$txtstream.WriteLine("   FONT-FAMILY: font-family: Cambria, serif;")
$txtstream.WriteLine("   FONT-SIZE: 12px;")
$txtstream.WriteLine("   text-align: left;")
$txtstream.WriteLine("   display:table-cell;")
$txtstream.WriteLine("   white-Space: nowrap;")
$txtstream.WriteLine("}")
$txtstream.WriteLine("h1 {")
$txtstream.WriteLine("color: antiquewhite;")
$txtstream.WriteLine("text-shadow: 1px 1px 1px black;")
```

```
$txtstream.WriteLine("padding: 3px;")
$txtstream.WriteLine("text-align: center;")
$txtstream.WriteLine("box-shadow: inset 2px 2px 5px rgba(0,0,0,0.5), inset -2px -2px 5px rgba(255,255,255,0.5)")
$txtstream.WriteLine("}")
$txtstream.WriteLine("</style>")
```

COLORED TEXT

```
$txtstream.WriteLine("<style type='text/css'>")
$txtstream.WriteLine("th")
$txtstream.WriteLine("{")
$txtstream.WriteLine("   COLOR: darkred;")
$txtstream.WriteLine("   BACKGROUND-COLOR: #eeeeee;")
$txtstream.WriteLine("   FONT-FAMILY:font-family: Cambria, serif;")
$txtstream.WriteLine("   FONT-SIZE: 12px;")
$txtstream.WriteLine("   text-align: left;")
$txtstream.WriteLine("   white-Space: nowrap;")
$txtstream.WriteLine("}")
$txtstream.WriteLine("td")
$txtstream.WriteLine("{")
$txtstream.WriteLine("   COLOR: navy;")
$txtstream.WriteLine("   BACKGROUND-COLOR: #eeeeee;")
$txtstream.WriteLine("   FONT-FAMILY: font-family: Cambria, serif;")
$txtstream.WriteLine("   FONT-SIZE: 12px;")
$txtstream.WriteLine("   text-align: left;")
$txtstream.WriteLine("   white-Space: nowrap;")
$txtstream.WriteLine("}")
$txtstream.WriteLine("div")
$txtstream.WriteLine("{")
$txtstream.WriteLine("   COLOR: white;")
$txtstream.WriteLine("   BACKGROUND-COLOR: navy;")
$txtstream.WriteLine("   FONT-FAMILY: font-family: Cambria, serif;")
```

```
$txtstream.WriteLine("    FONT-SIZE: 10px;")
$txtstream.WriteLine("    text-align: left;")
$txtstream.WriteLine("    white-Space: nowrap;")
$txtstream.WriteLine("}")
$txtstream.WriteLine("span")
$txtstream.WriteLine("{")
$txtstream.WriteLine("    COLOR: white;")
$txtstream.WriteLine("    BACKGROUND-COLOR: navy;")
$txtstream.WriteLine("    FONT-FAMILY: font-family: Cambria, serif;")
$txtstream.WriteLine("    FONT-SIZE: 10px;")
$txtstream.WriteLine("    text-align: left;")
$txtstream.WriteLine("    white-Space: nowrap;")
$txtstream.WriteLine("    display:inline-block;")
$txtstream.WriteLine("    width: 100%;")
$txtstream.WriteLine("}")
$txtstream.WriteLine("textarea")
$txtstream.WriteLine("{")
$txtstream.WriteLine("    COLOR: white;")
$txtstream.WriteLine("    BACKGROUND-COLOR: navy;")
$txtstream.WriteLine("    FONT-FAMILY: font-family: Cambria, serif;")
$txtstream.WriteLine("    FONT-SIZE: 10px;")
$txtstream.WriteLine("    text-align: left;")
$txtstream.WriteLine("    white-Space: nowrap;")
$txtstream.WriteLine("    width: 100%;")
$txtstream.WriteLine("}")
$txtstream.WriteLine("select")
$txtstream.WriteLine("{")
$txtstream.WriteLine("    COLOR: white;")
$txtstream.WriteLine("    BACKGROUND-COLOR: navy;")
$txtstream.WriteLine("    FONT-FAMILY: font-family: Cambria, serif;")
$txtstream.WriteLine("    FONT-SIZE: 10px;")
$txtstream.WriteLine("    text-align: left;")
$txtstream.WriteLine("    white-Space: nowrap;")
```

```
$txtstream.WriteLine("    width: 100%;")
$txtstream.WriteLine("}")
$txtstream.WriteLine("input")
$txtstream.WriteLine("{")
$txtstream.WriteLine("    COLOR: white;")
$txtstream.WriteLine("    BACKGROUND-COLOR: navy;")
$txtstream.WriteLine("    FONT-FAMILY: font-family: Cambria, serif;")
$txtstream.WriteLine("    FONT-SIZE: 12px;")
$txtstream.WriteLine("    text-align: left;")
$txtstream.WriteLine("    display:table-cell;")
$txtstream.WriteLine("    white-Space: nowrap;")
$txtstream.WriteLine("}")
$txtstream.WriteLine("h1 {")
$txtstream.WriteLine("color: antiquewhite;")
$txtstream.WriteLine("text-shadow: 1px 1px 1px black;")
$txtstream.WriteLine("padding: 3px;")
$txtstream.WriteLine("text-align: center;")
$txtstream.WriteLine("box-shadow: inset 2px 2px 5px rgba(0,0,0,0.5), inset -
2px -2px 5px rgba(255,255,255,0.5)")
$txtstream.WriteLine("}")
$txtstream.WriteLine("</style>")
```

OSCILLATING ROW COLORS

```
$txtstream.WriteLine("<style>")
$txtstream.WriteLine("th")
$txtstream.WriteLine("{")
$txtstream.WriteLine("    COLOR: white;")
$txtstream.WriteLine("    BACKGROUND-COLOR: navy;")
$txtstream.WriteLine("    FONT-FAMILY:font-family: Cambria, serif;")
$txtstream.WriteLine("    FONT-SIZE: 12px;")
```

```
$txtstream.WriteLine("   text-align: left;")
$txtstream.WriteLine("   white-Space: nowrap;")
$txtstream.WriteLine("}")
$txtstream.WriteLine("td")
$txtstream.WriteLine("{")
$txtstream.WriteLine("   COLOR: navy;")
$txtstream.WriteLine("   FONT-FAMILY: font-family: Cambria, serif;")
$txtstream.WriteLine("   FONT-SIZE: 12px;")
$txtstream.WriteLine("   text-align: left;")
$txtstream.WriteLine("   white-Space: nowrap;")
$txtstream.WriteLine("}")
$txtstream.WriteLine("div")
$txtstream.WriteLine("{")
$txtstream.WriteLine("   COLOR: navy;")
$txtstream.WriteLine("   FONT-FAMILY: font-family: Cambria, serif;")
$txtstream.WriteLine("   FONT-SIZE: 12px;")
$txtstream.WriteLine("   text-align: left;")
$txtstream.WriteLine("   white-Space: nowrap;")
$txtstream.WriteLine("}")
$txtstream.WriteLine("span")
$txtstream.WriteLine("{")
$txtstream.WriteLine("   COLOR: navy;")
$txtstream.WriteLine("   FONT-FAMILY: font-family: Cambria, serif;")
$txtstream.WriteLine("   FONT-SIZE: 12px;")
$txtstream.WriteLine("   text-align: left;")
$txtstream.WriteLine("   white-Space: nowrap;")
$txtstream.WriteLine("   width: 100%;")
$txtstream.WriteLine("}")
$txtstream.WriteLine("textarea")
$txtstream.WriteLine("{")
$txtstream.WriteLine("   COLOR: navy;")
$txtstream.WriteLine("   FONT-FAMILY: font-family: Cambria, serif;")
$txtstream.WriteLine("   FONT-SIZE: 12px;")
```

```
$txtstream.WriteLine("    text-align: left;")
$txtstream.WriteLine("    white-Space: nowrap;")
$txtstream.WriteLine("    display:inline-block;")
$txtstream.WriteLine("    width: 100%;")
$txtstream.WriteLine("}")
$txtstream.WriteLine("select")
$txtstream.WriteLine("{")
$txtstream.WriteLine("    COLOR: navy;")
$txtstream.WriteLine("    FONT-FAMILY: font-family: Cambria, serif;")
$txtstream.WriteLine("    FONT-SIZE: 10px;")
$txtstream.WriteLine("    text-align: left;")
$txtstream.WriteLine("    white-Space: nowrap;")
$txtstream.WriteLine("    display:inline-block;")
$txtstream.WriteLine("    width: 100%;")
$txtstream.WriteLine("}")
$txtstream.WriteLine("input")
$txtstream.WriteLine("{")
$txtstream.WriteLine("    COLOR: navy;")
$txtstream.WriteLine("    FONT-FAMILY: font-family: Cambria, serif;")
$txtstream.WriteLine("    FONT-SIZE: 12px;")
$txtstream.WriteLine("    text-align: left;")
$txtstream.WriteLine("    display:table-cell;")
$txtstream.WriteLine("    white-Space: nowrap;")
$txtstream.WriteLine("}")
$txtstream.WriteLine("h1 {")
$txtstream.WriteLine("color: antiquewhite;")
$txtstream.WriteLine("text-shadow: 1px 1px 1px black;")
$txtstream.WriteLine("padding: 3px;")
$txtstream.WriteLine("text-align: center;")
$txtstream.WriteLine("box-shadow: inset 2px 2px 5px rgba(0,0,0,0.5), inset -
2px -2px 5px rgba(255,255,255,0.5)")
$txtstream.WriteLine("}")
$txtstream.WriteLine("tr:nth-child(even){background-color:#f2f2f2;}")
```

```
$txtstream.WriteLine("tr:nth-child(odd){background-color:#cccccc;
color:#f2f2f2;}")
$txtstream.WriteLine("</style>")
```

GHOST DECORATED

```
$txtstream.WriteLine("<style type='text/css'>")
$txtstream.WriteLine("th")
$txtstream.WriteLine("{")
$txtstream.WriteLine("   COLOR: black;")
$txtstream.WriteLine("   BACKGROUND-COLOR: white;")
$txtstream.WriteLine("   FONT-FAMILY:font-family: Cambria, serif;")
$txtstream.WriteLine("   FONT-SIZE: 12px;")
$txtstream.WriteLine("   text-align: left;")
$txtstream.WriteLine("   white-Space: nowrap;")
$txtstream.WriteLine("}")
$txtstream.WriteLine("td")
$txtstream.WriteLine("{")
$txtstream.WriteLine("   COLOR: black;")
$txtstream.WriteLine("   BACKGROUND-COLOR: white;")
$txtstream.WriteLine("   FONT-FAMILY: font-family: Cambria, serif;")
$txtstream.WriteLine("   FONT-SIZE: 12px;")
$txtstream.WriteLine("   text-align: left;")
$txtstream.WriteLine("   white-Space: nowrap;")
$txtstream.WriteLine("}")
$txtstream.WriteLine("div")
$txtstream.WriteLine("{")
$txtstream.WriteLine("   COLOR: black;")
$txtstream.WriteLine("   BACKGROUND-COLOR: white;")
$txtstream.WriteLine("   FONT-FAMILY: font-family: Cambria, serif;")
$txtstream.WriteLine("   FONT-SIZE: 10px;")
$txtstream.WriteLine("   text-align: left;")
$txtstream.WriteLine("   white-Space: nowrap;")
```

```
$txtstream.WriteLine("}")
$txtstream.WriteLine("span")
$txtstream.WriteLine("{")
$txtstream.WriteLine("   COLOR: black;")
$txtstream.WriteLine("   BACKGROUND-COLOR: white;")
$txtstream.WriteLine("   FONT-FAMILY: font-family: Cambria, serif;")
$txtstream.WriteLine("   FONT-SIZE: 10px;")
$txtstream.WriteLine("   text-align: left;")
$txtstream.WriteLine("   white-Space: nowrap;")
$txtstream.WriteLine("   display:inline-block;")
$txtstream.WriteLine("   width: 100%;")
$txtstream.WriteLine("}")
$txtstream.WriteLine("textarea")
$txtstream.WriteLine("{")
$txtstream.WriteLine("   COLOR: black;")
$txtstream.WriteLine("   BACKGROUND-COLOR: white;")
$txtstream.WriteLine("   FONT-FAMILY: font-family: Cambria, serif;")
$txtstream.WriteLine("   FONT-SIZE: 10px;")
$txtstream.WriteLine("   text-align: left;")
$txtstream.WriteLine("   white-Space: nowrap;")
$txtstream.WriteLine("   width: 100%;")
$txtstream.WriteLine("}")
$txtstream.WriteLine("select")
$txtstream.WriteLine("{")
$txtstream.WriteLine("   COLOR: black;")
$txtstream.WriteLine("   BACKGROUND-COLOR: white;")
$txtstream.WriteLine("   FONT-FAMILY: font-family: Cambria, serif;")
$txtstream.WriteLine("   FONT-SIZE: 10px;")
$txtstream.WriteLine("   text-align: left;")
$txtstream.WriteLine("   white-Space: nowrap;")
$txtstream.WriteLine("   width: 100%;")
$txtstream.WriteLine("}")
$txtstream.WriteLine("input")
```

```
$txtstream.WriteLine("{")
$txtstream.WriteLine("    COLOR: black;")
$txtstream.WriteLine("    BACKGROUND-COLOR: white;")
$txtstream.WriteLine("    FONT-FAMILY: font-family: Cambria, serif;")
$txtstream.WriteLine("    FONT-SIZE: 12px;")
$txtstream.WriteLine("    text-align: left;")
$txtstream.WriteLine("    display:table-cell;")
$txtstream.WriteLine("    white-Space: nowrap;")
$txtstream.WriteLine("}")
$txtstream.WriteLine("h1 {")
$txtstream.WriteLine("color: antiquewhite;")
$txtstream.WriteLine("text-shadow: 1px 1px 1px black;")
$txtstream.WriteLine("padding: 3px;")
$txtstream.WriteLine("text-align: center;")
$txtstream.WriteLine("box-shadow: inset 2px 2px 5px rgba(0,0,0,0.5), inset -2px -2px 5px rgba(255,255,255,0.5)")
$txtstream.WriteLine("}")
$txtstream.WriteLine("</style>")
```

3D

```
$txtstream.WriteLine("<style type='text/css'>")
$txtstream.WriteLine("body")
$txtstream.WriteLine("{")
$txtstream.WriteLine("    PADDING-RIGHT: 0px;")
$txtstream.WriteLine("    PADDING-LEFT: 0px;")
$txtstream.WriteLine("    PADDING-BOTTOM: 0px;")
$txtstream.WriteLine("    MARGIN: 0px;")
$txtstream.WriteLine("    COLOR: #333;")
$txtstream.WriteLine("    PADDING-TOP: 0px;")
$txtstream.WriteLine("        FONT-FAMILY: verdana, arial, helvetica, sans-serif;")
```

```
$txtstream.WriteLine("}")
$txtstream.WriteLine("table")
$txtstream.WriteLine("{")
$txtstream.WriteLine("   BORDER-RIGHT: #999999 3px solid;")
$txtstream.WriteLine("   PADDING-RIGHT: 6px;")
$txtstream.WriteLine("   PADDING-LEFT: 6px;")
$txtstream.WriteLine("   FONT-WEIGHT: Bold;")
$txtstream.WriteLine("   FONT-SIZE: 14px;")
$txtstream.WriteLine("   PADDING-BOTTOM: 6px;")
$txtstream.WriteLine("   COLOR: Peru;")
$txtstream.WriteLine("   LINE-HEIGHT: 14px;")
$txtstream.WriteLine("   PADDING-TOP: 6px;")
$txtstream.WriteLine("   BORDER-BOTTOM: #999 1px solid;")
$txtstream.WriteLine("   BACKGROUND-COLOR: #eeeeee;")
$txtstream.WriteLine("      FONT-FAMILY: verdana, arial, helvetica, sans-serif;")
$txtstream.WriteLine("   FONT-SIZE: 12px;")
$txtstream.WriteLine("}")
$txtstream.WriteLine("th")
$txtstream.WriteLine("{")
$txtstream.WriteLine("   BORDER-RIGHT: #999999 3px solid;")
$txtstream.WriteLine("   PADDING-RIGHT: 6px;")
$txtstream.WriteLine("   PADDING-LEFT: 6px;")
$txtstream.WriteLine("   FONT-WEIGHT: Bold;")
$txtstream.WriteLine("   FONT-SIZE: 14px;")
$txtstream.WriteLine("   PADDING-BOTTOM: 6px;")
$txtstream.WriteLine("   COLOR: darkred;")
$txtstream.WriteLine("   LINE-HEIGHT: 14px;")
$txtstream.WriteLine("   PADDING-TOP: 6px;")
$txtstream.WriteLine("   BORDER-BOTTOM: #999 1px solid;")
$txtstream.WriteLine("   BACKGROUND-COLOR: #eeeeee;")
$txtstream.WriteLine("   FONT-FAMILY:font-family: Cambria, serif;")
$txtstream.WriteLine("   FONT-SIZE: 12px;")
```

```
$txtstream.WriteLine("   text-align: left;")
$txtstream.WriteLine("   white-Space: nowrap;")
$txtstream.WriteLine("}")
$txtstream.WriteLine(".th")
$txtstream.WriteLine("{")
$txtstream.WriteLine("   BORDER-RIGHT: #999999 2px solid;")
$txtstream.WriteLine("   PADDING-RIGHT: 6px;")
$txtstream.WriteLine("   PADDING-LEFT: 6px;")
$txtstream.WriteLine("   FONT-WEIGHT: Bold;")
$txtstream.WriteLine("   PADDING-BOTTOM: 6px;")
$txtstream.WriteLine("   COLOR: black;")
$txtstream.WriteLine("   PADDING-TOP: 6px;")
$txtstream.WriteLine("   BORDER-BOTTOM: #999 2px solid;")
$txtstream.WriteLine("   BACKGROUND-COLOR: #eeeeee;")
$txtstream.WriteLine("   FONT-FAMILY: font-family: Cambria, serif;")
$txtstream.WriteLine("   FONT-SIZE: 10px;")
$txtstream.WriteLine("   text-align: right;")
$txtstream.WriteLine("   white-Space: nowrap;")
$txtstream.WriteLine("}")
$txtstream.WriteLine("td")
$txtstream.WriteLine("{")
$txtstream.WriteLine("   BORDER-RIGHT: #999999 3px solid;")
$txtstream.WriteLine("   PADDING-RIGHT: 6px;")
$txtstream.WriteLine("   PADDING-LEFT: 6px;")
$txtstream.WriteLine("   FONT-WEIGHT: Normal;")
$txtstream.WriteLine("   PADDING-BOTTOM: 6px;")
$txtstream.WriteLine("   COLOR: navy;")
$txtstream.WriteLine("   LINE-HEIGHT: 14px;")
$txtstream.WriteLine("   PADDING-TOP: 6px;")
$txtstream.WriteLine("   BORDER-BOTTOM: #999 1px solid;")
$txtstream.WriteLine("   BACKGROUND-COLOR: #eeeeee;")
$txtstream.WriteLine("   FONT-FAMILY: font-family: Cambria, serif;")
$txtstream.WriteLine("   FONT-SIZE: 12px;")
```

```
$txtstream.WriteLine("   text-align: left;")
$txtstream.WriteLine("   white-Space: nowrap;")
$txtstream.WriteLine("}")
$txtstream.WriteLine("div")
$txtstream.WriteLine("{")
$txtstream.WriteLine("   BORDER-RIGHT: #999999 3px solid;")
$txtstream.WriteLine("   PADDING-RIGHT: 6px;")
$txtstream.WriteLine("   PADDING-LEFT: 6px;")
$txtstream.WriteLine("   FONT-WEIGHT: Normal;")
$txtstream.WriteLine("   PADDING-BOTTOM: 6px;")
$txtstream.WriteLine("   COLOR: white;")
$txtstream.WriteLine("   PADDING-TOP: 6px;")
$txtstream.WriteLine("   BORDER-BOTTOM: #999 1px solid;")
$txtstream.WriteLine("   BACKGROUND-COLOR: navy;")
$txtstream.WriteLine("   FONT-FAMILY: font-family: Cambria, serif;")
$txtstream.WriteLine("   FONT-SIZE: 10px;")
$txtstream.WriteLine("   text-align: left;")
$txtstream.WriteLine("   white-Space: nowrap;")
$txtstream.WriteLine("}")
$txtstream.WriteLine("span")
$txtstream.WriteLine("{")
$txtstream.WriteLine("   BORDER-RIGHT: #999999 3px solid;")
$txtstream.WriteLine("   PADDING-RIGHT: 3px;")
$txtstream.WriteLine("   PADDING-LEFT: 3px;")
$txtstream.WriteLine("   FONT-WEIGHT: Normal;")
$txtstream.WriteLine("   PADDING-BOTTOM: 3px;")
$txtstream.WriteLine("   COLOR: white;")
$txtstream.WriteLine("   PADDING-TOP: 3px;")
$txtstream.WriteLine("   BORDER-BOTTOM: #999 1px solid;")
$txtstream.WriteLine("   BACKGROUND-COLOR: navy;")
$txtstream.WriteLine("   FONT-FAMILY: font-family: Cambria, serif;")
$txtstream.WriteLine("   FONT-SIZE: 10px;")
$txtstream.WriteLine("   text-align: left;")
```

```
$txtstream.WriteLine("    white-Space: nowrap;")
$txtstream.WriteLine("    display:inline-block;")
$txtstream.WriteLine("    width: 100%;")
$txtstream.WriteLine("}")
$txtstream.WriteLine("textarea")
$txtstream.WriteLine("{")
$txtstream.WriteLine("    BORDER-RIGHT: #999999 3px solid;")
$txtstream.WriteLine("    PADDING-RIGHT: 3px;")
$txtstream.WriteLine("    PADDING-LEFT: 3px;")
$txtstream.WriteLine("    FONT-WEIGHT: Normal;")
$txtstream.WriteLine("    PADDING-BOTTOM: 3px;")
$txtstream.WriteLine("    COLOR: white;")
$txtstream.WriteLine("    PADDING-TOP: 3px;")
$txtstream.WriteLine("    BORDER-BOTTOM: #999 1px solid;")
$txtstream.WriteLine("    BACKGROUND-COLOR: navy;")
$txtstream.WriteLine("    FONT-FAMILY: font-family: Cambria, serif;")
$txtstream.WriteLine("    FONT-SIZE: 10px;")
$txtstream.WriteLine("    text-align: left;")
$txtstream.WriteLine("    white-Space: nowrap;")
$txtstream.WriteLine("    width: 100%;")
$txtstream.WriteLine("}")
$txtstream.WriteLine("select")
$txtstream.WriteLine("{")
$txtstream.WriteLine("    BORDER-RIGHT: #999999 3px solid;")
$txtstream.WriteLine("    PADDING-RIGHT: 6px;")
$txtstream.WriteLine("    PADDING-LEFT: 6px;")
$txtstream.WriteLine("    FONT-WEIGHT: Normal;")
$txtstream.WriteLine("    PADDING-BOTTOM: 6px;")
$txtstream.WriteLine("    COLOR: white;")
$txtstream.WriteLine("    PADDING-TOP: 6px;")
$txtstream.WriteLine("    BORDER-BOTTOM: #999 1px solid;")
$txtstream.WriteLine("    BACKGROUND-COLOR: navy;")
$txtstream.WriteLine("    FONT-FAMILY: font-family: Cambria, serif;")
```

```
$txtstream.WriteLine("   FONT-SIZE: 10px;")
$txtstream.WriteLine("   text-align: left;")
$txtstream.WriteLine("   white-Space: nowrap;")
$txtstream.WriteLine("   width: 100%;")
$txtstream.WriteLine("}")
$txtstream.WriteLine("input")
$txtstream.WriteLine("{")
$txtstream.WriteLine("   BORDER-RIGHT: #999999 3px solid;")
$txtstream.WriteLine("   PADDING-RIGHT: 3px;")
$txtstream.WriteLine("   PADDING-LEFT: 3px;")
$txtstream.WriteLine("   FONT-WEIGHT: Bold;")
$txtstream.WriteLine("   PADDING-BOTTOM: 3px;")
$txtstream.WriteLine("   COLOR: white;")
$txtstream.WriteLine("   PADDING-TOP: 3px;")
$txtstream.WriteLine("   BORDER-BOTTOM: #999 1px solid;")
$txtstream.WriteLine("   BACKGROUND-COLOR: navy;")
$txtstream.WriteLine("   FONT-FAMILY: font-family: Cambria, serif;")
$txtstream.WriteLine("   FONT-SIZE: 12px;")
$txtstream.WriteLine("   text-align: left;")
$txtstream.WriteLine("   display:table-cell;")
$txtstream.WriteLine("   white-Space: nowrap;")
$txtstream.WriteLine("   width: 100%;")
$txtstream.WriteLine("}")
$txtstream.WriteLine("h1 {")
$txtstream.WriteLine("color: antiquewhite;")
$txtstream.WriteLine("text-shadow: 1px 1px 1px black;")
$txtstream.WriteLine("padding: 3px;")
$txtstream.WriteLine("text-align: center;")
$txtstream.WriteLine("box-shadow: inset 2px 2px 5px rgba(0,0,0,0.5), inset -
2px -2px 5px rgba(255,255,255,0.5)")
$txtstream.WriteLine("}")
$txtstream.WriteLine("</style>")
```

SHADOW BOX

```
$txtstream.WriteLine("<style type='text/css'>")
$txtstream.WriteLine("body")
$txtstream.WriteLine("{")
$txtstream.WriteLine("   PADDING-RIGHT: 0px;")
$txtstream.WriteLine("   PADDING-LEFT: 0px;")
$txtstream.WriteLine("   PADDING-BOTTOM: 0px;")
$txtstream.WriteLine("   MARGIN: 0px;")
$txtstream.WriteLine("   COLOR: #333;")
$txtstream.WriteLine("   PADDING-TOP: 0px;")
$txtstream.WriteLine("       FONT-FAMILY: verdana, arial, helvetica, sans-serif;")
$txtstream.WriteLine("}")
$txtstream.WriteLine("table")
$txtstream.WriteLine("{")
$txtstream.WriteLine("   BORDER-RIGHT: #999999 1px solid;")
$txtstream.WriteLine("   PADDING-RIGHT: 1px;")
$txtstream.WriteLine("   PADDING-LEFT: 1px;")
$txtstream.WriteLine("   PADDING-BOTTOM: 1px;")
$txtstream.WriteLine("   LINE-HEIGHT: 8px;")
$txtstream.WriteLine("   PADDING-TOP: 1px;")
$txtstream.WriteLine("   BORDER-BOTTOM: #999 1px solid;")
$txtstream.WriteLine("   BACKGROUND-COLOR: #eeeeee;")
$txtstream.WriteLine("
filter:progid:DXImageTransform.Microsoft.Shadow(color='silver',     Direction=135,
Strength=16)")
$txtstream.WriteLine("}")
$txtstream.WriteLine("th")
$txtstream.WriteLine("{")
$txtstream.WriteLine("   BORDER-RIGHT: #999999 3px solid;")
$txtstream.WriteLine("   PADDING-RIGHT: 6px;")
$txtstream.WriteLine("   PADDING-LEFT: 6px;")
```

```
$txtstream.WriteLine("   FONT-WEIGHT: Bold;")
$txtstream.WriteLine("   FONT-SIZE: 14px;")
$txtstream.WriteLine("   PADDING-BOTTOM: 6px;")
$txtstream.WriteLine("   COLOR: darkred;")
$txtstream.WriteLine("   LINE-HEIGHT: 14px;")
$txtstream.WriteLine("   PADDING-TOP: 6px;")
$txtstream.WriteLine("   BORDER-BOTTOM: #999 1px solid;")
$txtstream.WriteLine("   BACKGROUND-COLOR: #eeeeee;")
$txtstream.WriteLine("   FONT-FAMILY: font-family: Cambria, serif;")
$txtstream.WriteLine("   FONT-SIZE: 12px;")
$txtstream.WriteLine("   text-align: left;")
$txtstream.WriteLine("   white-Space: nowrap;")
$txtstream.WriteLine("}")
$txtstream.WriteLine(".th")
$txtstream.WriteLine("{")
$txtstream.WriteLine("   BORDER-RIGHT: #999999 2px solid;")
$txtstream.WriteLine("   PADDING-RIGHT: 6px;")
$txtstream.WriteLine("   PADDING-LEFT: 6px;")
$txtstream.WriteLine("   FONT-WEIGHT: Bold;")
$txtstream.WriteLine("   PADDING-BOTTOM: 6px;")
$txtstream.WriteLine("   COLOR: black;")
$txtstream.WriteLine("   PADDING-TOP: 6px;")
$txtstream.WriteLine("   BORDER-BOTTOM: #999 2px solid;")
$txtstream.WriteLine("   BACKGROUND-COLOR: #eeeeee;")
$txtstream.WriteLine("   FONT-FAMILY: font-family: Cambria, serif;")
$txtstream.WriteLine("   FONT-SIZE: 10px;")
$txtstream.WriteLine("   text-align: right;")
$txtstream.WriteLine("   white-Space: nowrap;")
$txtstream.WriteLine("}")
$txtstream.WriteLine("td")
$txtstream.WriteLine("{")
$txtstream.WriteLine("   BORDER-RIGHT: #999999 3px solid;")
$txtstream.WriteLine("   PADDING-RIGHT: 6px;")
```

```
$txtstream.WriteLine("    PADDING-LEFT: 6px;")
$txtstream.WriteLine("    FONT-WEIGHT: Normal;")
$txtstream.WriteLine("    PADDING-BOTTOM: 6px;")
$txtstream.WriteLine("    COLOR: navy;")
$txtstream.WriteLine("    LINE-HEIGHT: 14px;")
$txtstream.WriteLine("    PADDING-TOP: 6px;")
$txtstream.WriteLine("    BORDER-BOTTOM: #999 1px solid;")
$txtstream.WriteLine("    BACKGROUND-COLOR: #eeeeee;")
$txtstream.WriteLine("    FONT-FAMILY: font-family: Cambria, serif;")
$txtstream.WriteLine("    FONT-SIZE: 12px;")
$txtstream.WriteLine("    text-align: left;")
$txtstream.WriteLine("    white-Space: nowrap;")
$txtstream.WriteLine("}")
$txtstream.WriteLine("div")
$txtstream.WriteLine("{")
$txtstream.WriteLine("    BORDER-RIGHT: #999999 3px solid;")
$txtstream.WriteLine("    PADDING-RIGHT: 6px;")
$txtstream.WriteLine("    PADDING-LEFT: 6px;")
$txtstream.WriteLine("    FONT-WEIGHT: Normal;")
$txtstream.WriteLine("    PADDING-BOTTOM: 6px;")
$txtstream.WriteLine("    COLOR: white;")
$txtstream.WriteLine("    PADDING-TOP: 6px;")
$txtstream.WriteLine("    BORDER-BOTTOM: #999 1px solid;")
$txtstream.WriteLine("    BACKGROUND-COLOR: navy;")
$txtstream.WriteLine("    FONT-FAMILY: font-family: Cambria, serif;")
$txtstream.WriteLine("    FONT-SIZE: 10px;")
$txtstream.WriteLine("    text-align: left;")
$txtstream.WriteLine("    white-Space: nowrap;")
$txtstream.WriteLine("}")
$txtstream.WriteLine("span")
$txtstream.WriteLine("{")
$txtstream.WriteLine("    BORDER-RIGHT: #999999 3px solid;")
$txtstream.WriteLine("    PADDING-RIGHT: 3px;")
```

```
$txtstream.WriteLine("   PADDING-LEFT: 3px;")
$txtstream.WriteLine("   FONT-WEIGHT: Normal;")
$txtstream.WriteLine("   PADDING-BOTTOM: 3px;")
$txtstream.WriteLine("   COLOR: white;")
$txtstream.WriteLine("   PADDING-TOP: 3px;")
$txtstream.WriteLine("   BORDER-BOTTOM: #999 1px solid;")
$txtstream.WriteLine("   BACKGROUND-COLOR: navy;")
$txtstream.WriteLine("   FONT-FAMILY: font-family: Cambria, serif;")
$txtstream.WriteLine("   FONT-SIZE: 10px;")
$txtstream.WriteLine("   text-align: left;")
$txtstream.WriteLine("   white-Space: nowrap;")
$txtstream.WriteLine("   display: inline-block;")
$txtstream.WriteLine("   width: 100%;")
$txtstream.WriteLine("}")
$txtstream.WriteLine("textarea")
$txtstream.WriteLine("{")
$txtstream.WriteLine("   BORDER-RIGHT: #999999 3px solid;")
$txtstream.WriteLine("   PADDING-RIGHT: 3px;")
$txtstream.WriteLine("   PADDING-LEFT: 3px;")
$txtstream.WriteLine("   FONT-WEIGHT: Normal;")
$txtstream.WriteLine("   PADDING-BOTTOM: 3px;")
$txtstream.WriteLine("   COLOR: white;")
$txtstream.WriteLine("   PADDING-TOP: 3px;")
$txtstream.WriteLine("   BORDER-BOTTOM: #999 1px solid;")
$txtstream.WriteLine("   BACKGROUND-COLOR: navy;")
$txtstream.WriteLine("   FONT-FAMILY: font-family: Cambria, serif;")
$txtstream.WriteLine("   FONT-SIZE: 10px;")
$txtstream.WriteLine("   text-align: left;")
$txtstream.WriteLine("   white-Space: nowrap;")
$txtstream.WriteLine("   width: 100%;")
$txtstream.WriteLine("}")
$txtstream.WriteLine("select")
$txtstream.WriteLine("{")
```

```
$txtstream.WriteLine("    BORDER-RIGHT: #999999 3px solid;")
$txtstream.WriteLine("    PADDING-RIGHT: 6px;")
$txtstream.WriteLine("    PADDING-LEFT: 6px;")
$txtstream.WriteLine("    FONT-WEIGHT: Normal;")
$txtstream.WriteLine("    PADDING-BOTTOM: 6px;")
$txtstream.WriteLine("    COLOR: white;")
$txtstream.WriteLine("    PADDING-TOP: 6px;")
$txtstream.WriteLine("    BORDER-BOTTOM: #999 1px solid;")
$txtstream.WriteLine("    BACKGROUND-COLOR: navy;")
$txtstream.WriteLine("    FONT-FAMILY: font-family: Cambria, serif;")
$txtstream.WriteLine("    FONT-SIZE: 10px;")
$txtstream.WriteLine("    text-align: left;")
$txtstream.WriteLine("    white-Space: nowrap;")
$txtstream.WriteLine("    width: 100%;")
$txtstream.WriteLine("}")
$txtstream.WriteLine("input")
$txtstream.WriteLine("{")
$txtstream.WriteLine("    BORDER-RIGHT: #999999 3px solid;")
$txtstream.WriteLine("    PADDING-RIGHT: 3px;")
$txtstream.WriteLine("    PADDING-LEFT: 3px;")
$txtstream.WriteLine("    FONT-WEIGHT: Bold;")
$txtstream.WriteLine("    PADDING-BOTTOM: 3px;")
$txtstream.WriteLine("    COLOR: white;")
$txtstream.WriteLine("    PADDING-TOP: 3px;")
$txtstream.WriteLine("    BORDER-BOTTOM: #999 1px solid;")
$txtstream.WriteLine("    BACKGROUND-COLOR: navy;")
$txtstream.WriteLine("    FONT-FAMILY: font-family: Cambria, serif;")
$txtstream.WriteLine("    FONT-SIZE: 12px;")
$txtstream.WriteLine("    text-align: left;")
$txtstream.WriteLine("    display: table-cell;")
$txtstream.WriteLine("    white-Space: nowrap;")
$txtstream.WriteLine("    width: 100%;")
$txtstream.WriteLine("}")
```

```
$txtstream.WriteLine("h1 {")
$txtstream.WriteLine("color: antiquewhite;")
$txtstream.WriteLine("text-shadow: 1px 1px 1px black;")
$txtstream.WriteLine("padding: 3px;")
$txtstream.WriteLine("text-align: center;")
$txtstream.WriteLine("box-shadow: inset 2px 2px 5px rgba(0,0,0,0.5), inset -2px -2px 5px rgba(255,255,255,0.5)")
$txtstream.WriteLine("}")
$txtstream.WriteLine("</style>")
```

www.ingramcontent.com/pod-product-compliance
Lightning Source LLC
Chambersburg PA
CBHW031244050326
40690CB00007B/943